British Academy Occasional Paper · 8

History, Commemoration, and National Preoccupation: Trafalgar 1805–2005

Edited by

Holger Hoock

Published for THE BRITISH ACADEMY
by OXFORD UNIVERSITY PRESS

Oxford University Press, Great Clarendon Street, Oxford OX2 6DP
Oxford New York

Auckland Cape Town Dar es Salaam Hong Kong Karachi
Kuala Lumpur Madrid Melbourne Mexico City Nairobi
New Delhi Shanghai Taipei Toronto

With offices in
Argentina Austria Brazil Chile Czech Republic France Greece
Guatemala Hungary Italy Japan Poland Singapore
South Korea Switzerland Thailand Turkey Ukraine Vietnam

Published in the United States
by Oxford University Press Inc., New York

British Library Cataloguing in Publication Data
Data available

Library of Congress Cataloging in Publication Data
Data available

Typeset by
J&L Composition, Filey, North Yorkshire
Printed in Great Britain
on acid-free paper by
Antony Rowe Limited, Chippenham, Wiltshire

ISBN 978–0–19–726406–5

Contents

Illustrations

Notes on Contributors

Mark Connelly is Reader in Modern British History and Head of the School of History at the University of Kent. He is particularly interested in the image of the armed forces in British society and has worked extensively on war and memory. Publications include *The Great War, Memory and Ritual: Commemoration in the City and East London, 1916–1939* (2002), *We Can Take It! Britain and the Memory of the Second World War* (2004), and *Steady the Buffs! A Regiment, a Region, and the Great War* (2006).

Martin Daunton is Professor of Economic History at the University of Cambridge and Master of Trinity Hall, as well as President of the Royal Historical Society and a Trustee of the National Maritime Museum. His most recent works include a two-volume study of the politics of taxation in Britain since 1799 and a general economic history of Britain 1850–1950.

Peter Hicks is historian and chargé d'affaires internationales at the Fondation Napoléon, Paris and Visiting Research Fellow at the University of Bath. His recent Napoleonic publications include 'Hudson Lowe' in Michel Dancoisne-Martineau et al. (eds.), *Sainte-Hélène* (2005) and 'Regards sur la politique étrangère de la Grande-Bretagne, 1806–1815' in Thierry Lentz (ed.), *Napoléon et l'Europe* (2005).

Holger Hoock is Lecturer in British Cultural History and Director of the Interdisciplinary Research Centre 'Eighteenth-Century Worlds' at the University of Liverpool. His publications include *The King's Artists* (2003) and 'Nelson entombed: the military and naval pantheon in St Paul's Cathedral' in David Cannadine (ed.), *Admiral Lord Nelson: Context and Legacy* (2005). He was the research curator of 'Nelson & Napoléon' (National Maritime Museum, 2005). In 2006, he was awarded a Philip Leverhulme Prize for History.

Ludmilla Jordanova is Professor of Modern History at King's College, London and a Trustee of the National Portrait Gallery. Among her many books is *History in Practice* (2nd edition, 2006), which includes a discussion of public history. Her research concerns the ways in which portraits are used to construct individual and group identities. She is currently writing a book for Cambridge University Press on historians' use of visual and material evidence.

Margarette Lincoln is Director of Research and Planning at the National Maritime Museum, Greenwich and Visiting Fellow at Goldsmiths College, University of London. Recent books include *Representing the Navy: British Sea Power 1750–1815* (2002), and the catalogue for the Museum's special exhibition, *Nelson & Napoléon*, which she edited in 2005. Her book *Naval Wives and Mistresses 1745–1815*, a study of naval women and their social position within the context of Britain's growing imperial power, will be published in 2007.

John M. MacKenzie, professor emeritus at Lancaster, is the general editor of Manchester University Press's series Studies in Imperialism, has just completed a book on the Scots in South Africa, and is working on a project on the history of museums in the British Empire. Long interested in the concept of the hero, he delivered a Nelson lecture in London in 2004, published in David Cannadine (ed.), *Admiral Lord Nelson: Context and Legacy* (2005).

Bertrand Taithe is Professor of Cultural History at the University of Manchester. He has published extensively on war, medicine, commemoration, and citizenship, including *Citizenship and Wars: France in Turmoil 1870–1* (2001) and *Defeated Flesh: Welfare, Warfare, and the Making of Modern Britain* (1999), and on the French Empire (special issue of *French History*, 2006). His current research on turn of the century colonial warfare will lead to a monograph on war atrocities and humanitarianism in the French Sudan for Oxford University Press.

Colin White is Director of the Royal Naval Museum, and from 2001 to 2005 was Director, Trafalgar 200 at the National Maritime Museum, responsible for coordinating the Trafalgar Festival 2005. A lifelong historian of the Royal Navy in the 'long nineteenth century', he is widely recognized as an authority on Nelson's career and his posthumous reputation. His most recent books include the award-winning *Nelson: The New Letters* (2005) and *Nelson the Admiral* (2005).

Introduction

HOLGER HOOCK

This volume of essays arose out of a symposium held at the British Academy in January 2006, on the weekend after the bicentenary of the state funeral of Admiral Lord Nelson at St Paul's Cathedral and thus at the conclusion of a year which had seen hundreds of official, commercial, and popular events commemorating and celebrating the bicentenary of the Battle of Trafalgar and the death of Nelson. During 2005, in a variety of ways, we had been reminded of Nelson the public hero and the private man—from nearly thirty new or reissued books to TV documentaries, from regattas to parades, and from bell-ringing to tree planting. At many of the commemorative events, scripts appeared to cross-reference, overlap, and become conflated. For instance, there were battle re-enactments, among others, in the Solent, in the Royal Albert Hall, and at St Paul's Cathedral, all emphasizing similar elements and quoting the same words by Nelson again and again—including his last prayer, written just before the Battle of Trafalgar, which he took such care to have transmitted to posterity, so that it would become part of his legacy and legend.

Europe and the wider western world have known the 'cult of the centenary' at least since the late nineteenth century. In Britain, so-called 'round' anniversaries of political events have been commemorated since 1788—the centenary of the Glorious Revolution—and of battles since 1843, when the 200th anniversary of John Hamden's death after the skirmish at Chalgrove Field was marked by the erection of a monument. The word 'bicentenary' itself is first documented in the English language in 1862—the bicentenary of English Restoration Nonconformity.[1]

Historians soon developed an ambiguous attitude towards the anniversary business. In 1908, the Revd William Hunt, President of the Royal Historical Society, declared rather dismissively: 'We do not, as a rule, observe anniversaries. We should find it hard to draw a line between those that are worthy of commemoration and others; it would interrupt our regular

---

[1] Roland Edwin Quinault, 'The cult of the centenary, c.1784–1914', *Historical Research*, 71 (1998), 303–23, at 304, 313 (quotation), 309.

I

work, and such commemorations have been done to death.'[2] But the very same year, some of Hunt's liberal imperialist colleagues championed the commemoration of the bicentenary of the birth of Pitt, the Earl of Chatham, as the alleged founder of *Weltpolitik* and trans-oceanic imperialism.

Today, historians are increasingly concerning themselves with themes such as memory, commemoration, and memorialization, often in the context of 'public history', and they are themselves contributing to a 'commemorative effort' around anniversaries such as that of Trafalgar and Nelson's death. The changing manner of memorializing key moments in national history allows historians to study cultural meanings and interpretations of national identity. Since the 'Nelson phenomenon', the legend and cult of Horatio Nelson, began with Nelson himself, it lends itself to a *longue durée* approach. This is the approach taken in this collection of essays—not by any means in an attempt to be comprehensive, but rather by taking historical snapshots, as it were, in and around 1805, 1905, and 2005. At the symposium we wanted to step back and reflect systematically and critically on the notions of 'commemoration' and 'celebration' (and the distinction is one of the issues explored by several contributors to this volume) and on the previous year's Nelsonian events. Certain questions were raised: who drives the commemoration of historical anniversaries and to what ends? Which Nelson, or Nelson*s*—from the naval tactician and public hero to the private man of feeling—have been commemorated and have had a role in national memory over the past two centuries? There was also the question of identification: how does that complex process work across the interval of 100, now 200 years, and who identifies with Nelson today? Constructions of the past have been mobilized and contested within contemporary politics, and by different institutions, interest groups, and businesses over these past two centuries, and we asked how memoirs, history writing, visual and modern media and museums, institutions, and official and unofficial interests, contribute to keeping and shaping memory. Finally we explored what is, and what should be, the role of professional historians vis-à-vis such commemorations and celebrations.

The present volume assembles the revised versions of the papers delivered at the symposium along with three specially commissioned essays. In the opening chapter, Ludmilla Jordanova reflects critically on 'marking time'—the complex and interlinked notions of remembrance, celebration, honouring, and commemoration. She unpacks some of the assumptions

---

[2] William Hunt, 'Presidential Address: Observations on the Historical Association, the Advanced Historical Teaching (London) Fund, the Historical Congresses at Berlin and Saragossa, recent publications of Fellows and Society, and the progress of the Society', *Transactions of the Royal Historical Society*, 3rd series, 3 (1909), 18.

about periodization and the nature of historical agency bound up with commemoration and tackles the difficult notions of 'identification' and 'honouring'. Jordanova exhorts professional historians to subject all these to critical analysis when engaging with public history.

Following on from these theoretical and conceptual considerations, subsequent essays study particular Nelson commemorations. Colin White asks what the heroification of Nelson immediately after his death entailed. What conflicting images were created, in text and visual media, perhaps continuing the ways in which Nelson himself had manipulated his image during his lifetime? Contrasting official with popular commemoration, and exploring their interaction, White presents a nuanced picture of 'national' commemorations.

Moving forward a century, Bertrand Taithe explores the centenary of Trafalgar in 1905, not only from the British but especially from a French perspective. That year marked the shift from memory and narrative iteration at first hand to commemoration. Taithe analyses history and memory both from the perspective of 1905—in the contexts of the recent Entente Cordiale with Britain and the dismantling of the Napoleonic religious consensus—as well as of the subsequent historiography of that period. He explores the paradox of French participation in remembering defeat and concludes that—while going against the general thrust of French commemoration of 1805—French celebrations in 1905 fitted with a pattern of memorializing past conflicts. John MacKenzie then extends the perspective on 1905 into a British and imperial dimension and traces resonances and reverberations of the Nelson myth as an imperial and international hero in both Britain and Canada, ending with an exploration of the treatment of Nelson in twentieth-century international cinema.

The setting for the bicentenary in 2005 was, of course, again completely different from 1905. Britain had long lost its imperial status, and many Britons at least at the start of the bicentenary campaign appeared to know little about Nelson or Trafalgar. We attempted the first critical retrospective of the bicenentary season and asked how Nelson's heroism and the achievements of the Royal Navy played in modern Britain. Mark Connelly heroically discharged the daunting commission to attend a wide range of academic and public bicentenary events, monitored many more in the media, and interviewed several groups of (primarily young) people over the course of 2005, with the aim of exploring the current state of knowledge about, and national identification with, Nelson, Trafalgar, and Britain's maritime past. Connelly strikes a sceptical note on the long-term impact of 2005 on historical awareness: without direct state intervention in the National Curriculum, it appears difficult to see how the role of the navy, Nelson, and the sea can be more fully instilled in British life.

Two further essays were commissioned to round off this volume. Margarette Lincoln, as Director of Collections and Research, and Martin Daunton, as Trustee, of the National Maritime Museum in Greenwich, in their contribution reflect critically on the Museum's 2005 blockbuster exhibition 'Nelson & Napoléon'. They find and explain significant gaps between the intentions of Museum Trustees, management, and curators on the one hand, and public reception and responses on the other, with respect both to the composition of the exhibition audience and to 'meaning making'. Yet, concluding on a more optimistic note than Connelly, Daunton and Lincoln suggest that public responses to the 2005 anniversary indicate that Britain is beginning to take its maritime heritage more seriously, a process they expect will continue with the complex bicentenary of the abolition of the slave trade in 2007.

French reception of the fully bilingual exhibition 'Nelson & Napoléon' was limited, and—in parallel with much British coverage—in good part focused on questions of national identity in ways that ignored or undermined the organizers' intentions. In the epilogue to this collection, Peter Hicks, the British historian of the Parisian Fondation Napoléon, reflects on the absence of official commemoration in France of the Napoleonic bicentenaries. In an essay which resonates with Taithe's, Hicks discusses the complex role of Napoleon in French history, memory, and public history today.

Many contributors to this collection explicitly address the role and duty of the professional historian in critically analysing the multiple agendas served by commemorating historical anniversaries and in engaging with public history more generally. Jordanova asks the historical profession to take seriously its obligation to judge and appraise frankly historical phenomena and to re-present them to wide publics, always being aware of their own contributions to the 'commemorative effort'. Connelly reminds historians of the need to balance the demands of their professional discipline with the public demand for History 'as a repository of national triumphs and tragedies'. For Daunton and Lincoln the question of what should be commemorated, and how, raises complex questions about national identity and citizenship. And Hicks suggests that remembrance 'without enthusiasm' is possible and necessary as part of the responsible practice of public history, and that remembering a figure such as Napoleon ought best to occur in a European context.

It remains my pleasant duty to thank the British Academy for its generous intellectual and financial support throughout this project. I am grateful to its Fellows and Officers, and especially to the former Secretary, Peter Brown, for hosting the symposium in the splendid surroundings of Carlton

House Terrace. On behalf of all speakers and contributors I thank the Communications and Activities Committee, chaired by Professor John S. Morrill, for sponsoring the event, Michael Reade and his team from Public Events for organizing it with quite superb efficiency, and James Rivington and his team, as well as the copy editor, Dr Susan Milligan, for seeing this volume of essays through publication. We were privileged to have Professors John Morrill and Nicholas Rodger as congenial and effective chairs, and Dr Margarette Lincoln (National Maritime Museum), Professor Eric Evans (Lancaster), and Deidre Livingstone (SeaBritain 2005) as insightful discussants around the final roundtable. Thanks are also due to the institutions and individuals credited in the captions for permission to reproduce images.

I would like to thank especially all the contributors who with great commitment prepared for the symposium, spoke to their agreed briefs, and responded patiently first to the frequent demands and prompts of the convener, and subsequently to editorial suggestions and requests. I am very grateful to our challenging and responsive audience at the British Academy who practised with us 'public history' and encouraged us to seek to publish the results in this volume. Finally, I wish to thank Frances Macmillan for her editorial advice and her crucial assistance and support throughout the period when this volume was taking shape.

I.

Marking Time

LUDMILLA JORDANOVA

Marking time is the business of historians, who delineate and name historical periods, debate the nature of key figures, events, and turning points, make retrospective assessments of their significance, and draw the attention of their audiences to times past, to the passage of time, to time as a phenomenon. But historians possess no exclusive rights in these matters. On the contrary, marking time is part of everyday life: responses to births, marriages, and deaths, marking anniversaries, the celebration of symbolic moments, the remembrance of tragedy, whether individual or shared, all these are woven into the fabric of everyday existence, and have been so for many centuries. Indeed historians depend upon such quotidian experiences for source materials and inspiration. Increasingly, historians are engaging directly with themes such as memory, commemoration, and memorialization. At least in part they are doing so because of the growth of public history, a complex phenomenon that brings these apparently diverse forms of marking time together. The elaborate celebration of anniversaries, such as that of the death of Admiral Lord Nelson and the Battle of Trafalgar in 2005, may be understood as one aspect of a larger trend that I am evoking in the phrase 'marking time', and associating with the growth of interest in the linked phenomena of commemoration and public history. My essay is an exploration of these shifts in historical practice.[1]

The celebration of historical events is a feature of our times; it is a feature that insistently claims the attention of large swathes of the population, whether they like it or not. Products and advertising as well as the media are notable vehicles for bringing the past into the present. Marking time is big business. None of this is unproblematic. It is an important task for historians to analyse critically contemporary uses of the past, which are considerably more slippery than might appear at first sight. The Nelson extravaganza has provided an excellent opportunity for doing so, and a number of central

---

[1] It builds on some earlier work, for example: Ludmilla Jordanova, *History in Practice*, 2nd edn (London, 2006) and ead., 'Angels writing on the shoulders of time?', *Österreichische Zeitschrift für Geschichtswissenschaften*, 16 (2005), 11–26.

issues that are of the widest possible significance for the practice of history are evident. The nature of heroism, the cult of celebrity, and the role of a sense of nationhood are obvious examples of themes present in recent responses to Nelson that enjoy more general resonance. The appeal of anniversaries certainly invites careful scrutiny. I shall be just as concerned with a cluster of ideas—remembrance, celebration, honouring, and commemoration—that are used freely, perhaps too freely, and that have gathered rich emotional-cum-political significance. So much so that it feels faintly impertinent to subject them to sceptical analysis. Yet this is essential if historians are to retain and to develop further their professional obligation to be responsible, judicious commentators on what constitutes historical knowledge and the claims it may legitimately underwrite.

Perhaps these preliminary remarks sound a little stern; they are not intended to diminish the pleasure or any of the other emotions that 'celebration' of past figures and events is capable of generating. They are intended, however, to question the nature of such celebrations and to prompt reflection about the implications of the commercialism that is bound up with them. These arguments need to be developed through specific examples. Accordingly I will begin with some reflections on Nelson, or rather on Nelson as he has recently been re-presented, re-imagined, re-packaged. Yet in doing so I acknowledge how very old many of the familiar stories, images, and tropes are. It has unfortunately become rather trite to invoke the notion of self-fashioning, yet its pertinence is undeniable.[2] The 'Nelson' phenomenon began, after all, with the man himself, and hence is apt for a *longue durée* approach. Others took up the task of constructing his identity with alacrity, during his lifetime and immediately afterwards, and there does not seem to have been a time when Nelson's heroic status faded from public view. It has been kept alive in a relatively low-key way by, for example, pub signs, and especially in Norfolk he is ubiquitous.[3] A secondary school textbook in the Lively History series published in 1972 set out the possibilities for local study on Nelson and Trafalgar. It showed a photograph of a North Norfolk inn sign depicting him with the word 'hero' above the portrait, and invited pupils to find 'street names, place names, monuments and plaques in your home county [that] commemorate Nelson, Trafalgar and other naval victories of the period'. The historical significance of Nelson is briefly explained: 'Nelson was a very great admiral. If you study further the

[2] Stephen Greenblatt, *Renaissance Self-Fashioning: From More to Shakespeare* (Chicago, 1980) is widely considered a classic statement.
[3] It is possible to purchase at the Norwich Castle Museum a Nelson mug and also a small-format short life: David Williams, *Horatio Nelson: Vice Admiral of the White* (Dereham, Norfolk, 2000).

story of his life and career you will discover why he was commemorated with such splendour in the cities and towns of the British Isles and how he came to deserve the description "Hero".'[4]

This publication neatly illustrates an important point—figures and events are constantly moving in and out of focus. Anniversaries serve to bring them into the sharpest focus, but in doing so they draw on experiences that are already present, if in a more blurred fashion. Much of the past that is in the public domain possesses such a fluid status; it is a matter of some interest how chunks of history temporarily lose their indistinct, background qualities, and capture the imagination and interest of broad audiences. Who drives such shifts, for example? In whose interests do they occur? Why are some figures more successful than others when catapulted into prominence? It is hardly possible in a short essay to provide answers to such complex questions, but it may be feasible to suggest some ways of considering them.

A collaboration between the BBC and the National Portrait Gallery, London, which resulted in a television series and a book, *Great Britons*, brought Nelson into particularly crisp focus since he came fifth in the poll to find 'our favourite Britons—the top 100'. There he came after Elizabeth I, William Shakespeare, Oliver Cromwell, and Isaac Newton, but higher than Charles Darwin and Winston Churchill.[5] Such exercises in cultivating a broad sense of national heroism certainly mobilize long-established idioms; they remain capable of drawing public attention to the issues around marking time. In the process they provide historians with helpful insights. The *Great Britons* project reveals four points in particular. First, it indicates how crucial it is to have material objects—portraits and commemorative ceramics, for example—through which people and events are remembered. In Nelson's case there was a range of portraits produced during his lifetime, a number of death scenes, illustrations of the funeral, satirical prints, mugs, jugs, and so on. Then as now distinct audiences and markets were catered for. The capacity to reproduce recognizable images was vital, and extended to paintings, which were often copied without losing their aura. Second, it acknowledges that we are in the territory of myth. This is a difficult concept, since it is sometimes used to mean a fabricated account, and by that token, is pejorative. But myth is more properly understood as a

---

[4] Philip A. Sauvain, *Empire, City and Industry (1789–1901)*, Lively History 3 (Amersham, Bucks, 1972), p. 5. For an acute recent discussion of Nelson's heroism see Kathleen Wilson, 'How Nelson became a hero', *The Historian*, 87 (2005), 6–17.

[5] John Cooper, *Great Britons: The Great Debate* (London, 2002), see pp. 8–9 for 'Our favourite Britons—the top 100'. The section on Nelson, including essays by Lucy Moore and John Cooper and numerous illustrations, is on pp. 81–95.

dense, powerfully delineated story that contains familiar patterns and clear significance for both individuals and groups. Yet the relationships between history and myth are intricate. Academic history dedicates itself to interpreting and evaluating, not reproducing myth, hence one of the challenges of public history, which often mobilizes myth in order to gain attention. In speaking about Nelson in relation to myth, *Great Britons* acknowledges the complexities of his life and legacy.[6] Third, the project reveals the importance of what I call 'cultural effort', the elaborate work that goes into forging reputations, images, artefacts, texts, displays, and so on.[7] Historians not only study such effort, they exert it themselves, and this is why it is essential that a critical discourse is now created around phenomena in which we, historians, are implicated and from which we are sometimes direct beneficiaries. Fourth, *Great Britons* acknowledges, if with a light touch, that moral questions are involved. Nelson had a mistress and an illegitimate child, and did not conceal these facts. Furthermore he manifested, in John Cooper's happy phrase, 'creative insubordination'.[8] Thus it becomes possible to argue that Nelson's faults directly contributed to his heroism. This is a matter of some moment, given the idiom of 'celebration' that surrounds the marking of anniversaries. What does it mean to *celebrate* such a figure and their doings, as opposed, say, to recognizing, remembering, or commemorating them?

It is tempting to believe that the main meaning of 'celebration' here involves having a good time, a jolly tribute to times past. In everyday life, anniversaries and parties do indeed go hand in hand—both, after all, involve conspicuous consumption. Perhaps we should consider two other connotations of 'celebrate'. If, following a death, the notion of 'celebrating' the life that preceded it is invoked, this is hardly intended to convey the activity of partying. Rather, it suggests gripping, respectfully, the elaborate phenomenon that is a life, judging it, giving it its due. The associations here, then, go in a rather different direction; weighing up rather than having fun. The religious connotations of celebration should also be acknowledged. Priests, after all, 'celebrate' the mass: they are permitted to perform, repeatedly and for other believers, actions supercharged with holy significance. Here too we leave 'getting and spending' and partying behind for sacred ritual.[9] In contemporary practices, these three senses of celebration are blended and perhaps confused. It is vital not to mistake entertainment for

---

[6] Cooper, *Great Britons*, e.g. p. 84.

[7] Ludmilla Jordanova, *Nature Displayed: Gender, Science and Medicine 1760–1820* (Harlow, Essex, 1999), ch. 1.

[8] Cooper, *Great Britons*, p. 87.

[9] The phrase 'getting and spending' may be found as a chapter heading in Roy Porter's *English Society in the Eighteenth Century* (Harmondsworth, 1982), which stressed the central role that consumption played in eighteenth-century England.

giving a historical phenomenon its due or for performing a profound ritual. The last two forms of celebration are among the most important tasks historians undertake. After all, historians enjoy privileged access to precious sources; they are allowed to bear witness on behalf of others to the intricacies of the past; they assist in making the past usable.

The celebration of the 200th anniversary of Nelson's death was a complex matter involving many institutions, interest groups, and businesses; professional historians and academic organizations were among them. Anniversaries attract attention, even if that attention is of diverse kinds. Sometimes it is nakedly commercial, as in the case of a twelve-night cruise organized around 'Nelson—Man and Legend' that took in Malta, Sicily, Naples, Sardinia, Elba, Corsica, Minorca, Motril and Granada, and the battle sites of Trafalgar and Cadiz. Such a spring Mediterranean cruise could, of course, be billed in a number of ways. The itinerary mentions the links that most of the places have with Nelson (and many with Napoleon); it does so in a manner that hints at the magic to be derived from visiting locations associated with Nelson and having them brought to life by the guest speaker, whose institutional affiliation and publication on Nelson are detailed. Indeed the cruise is described as 'mark[ing] the bicentenary of nelson's (sic) death'. The beginning of the pitch is as follows: 'In the BBC's recent pole (sic) to find the greatest ever Briton, Nelson faired (sic) highly and it is a great testament to his contribution to his country that even two hundred years after his death he is still so highly regarded. He has a very special place in our maritime history, and our commemorative cruise . . .'.[10] Despite the mistakes, the writing is cunning in that it yokes together Nelson and his country, the nation's maritime history, and a company that runs cruises. Potential patrons are enfolded in Britain's past; they are invited to re-enact specific aspects of it as part of the bicentenary celebrations, while being given a sense that they will gain authoritative knowledge in the process. We might say that anniversaries allow members of the general public to have vicarious historical experiences (in this case, at their own, very considerable, expense).

Rich historical figures and events can attract successfully many different types of attention. Or perhaps it is the other way round. Interest groups, attention seekers, search for and find resources in the past that feed their needs and desires. Feminist historians have frequently sought the gender angle, for example. It is deemed valuable to show how groups and individuals that may have been under-studied, undervalued, under-recognized, are in fact noteworthy, although the comparative judgements such claims imply

---

[10] I refer to pp. 6–7 of the 2004 brochure advertising a range of cruises by the following company: www.noble-caledonia.co.uk.

(x is as noteworthy as y), are never easily secured. Emma Hamilton, wife of Sir William Hamilton and Nelson's mistress, was receiving considerable historical attention long before the recent bicentenary. Her association with the artist George Romney, who painted her many times, and the growing scholarly interest in her husband as a formidable collector and patron, have both helped.[11] Furthermore, Nelson's colourful personal life fits nicely with the intense curiosity about the lives of celebrities which, while hardly new, is now being fed in ever more inventive ways by the media. That there is also a race perspective on the Nelson anniversary is striking. For example, during Black History Month (October), *The Independent* ran an article about 'the seamen who did their duty for Nelson and England 200 years ago [who] came from many nations and races, and included black men from the West Indies'. It drew readers' attention to a historical phenomenon of which many, perhaps most, would have been unaware. The article is designed to give these men their due. The mere fact that such an article appeared (and an exhibition to which it refers) links the anniversary with a theme of considerable importance in contemporary life—the contribution made by people born outside Britain to symbolically important national activities. Although about 'foreigners on the "Victory" ', the main heading reads 'The Black Heroes of Trafalgar', which makes it clear that particular value is being given to a specific group.[12]

What is not spelled out in the *Independent* article, although it is assumed, is the potential identification of (some) readers with these heroes. Like the very concept of an annual Black History Month or Women's Day, the article was performing a number of operations simultaneously. My argument is that for an understanding of these operations, 'identification' is a useful idea. A complex notion, for which we are indebted to psychoanalytic theory and practice, in lay usage it loosely expresses a sense of connection that individuals and groups can find in others, and in representations of others, who are, somehow, 'like' them. Yet we do well to remind ourselves of its psychoanalytic definition: a 'psychological process whereby the subject assimilates an aspect, property or attribute of the other and is transformed, wholly or partially, after the model the other provides. It is by means of a series of identifications that the personality is constituted and specified.'[13] Two aspects of this understanding of 'identification' stand out. First, it refers

[11] See, for example, Ian Jenkins and Kim Sloan (eds), *Vases and Volcanoes: Sir William Hamilton and His Collection* (London, 1996); Marcia Pointon, *Strategies for Showing: Women, Possession and Representation in English Visual Culture 1665–1800* (Oxford, 1997), ch. 5; Alex Kidson, *George Romney 1734–1802* (London, 2002).
[12] Colin Brown, 'The black heroes of Trafalgar', *The Independent*, 19 October 2005, 10–11.
[13] Jean Laplanche and Jean-Bertrand Pontalis, *The Language of Psychoanalysis* (London, 1973), pp. 205–8, definition at p. 205.

to a relationship between self and *other*; this should alert us to the problems of assuming that the perception of 'likeness' is at all straightforward. Second, these are dynamic processes, from which it follows that the subject is active, and that permanent traits, those deriving from a chromosomal profile, for instance, hardly determine those processes in any simple or direct manner. Jean Laplanche and Jean-Bertrand Pontalis recognized that 'identification' has a life beyond psychoanalysis, noting its overlap in everyday usage with terms such as imitation, empathy, sympathy, mental contagion, and projection.[14] At the moment it also connects with ideas of emulation and with the linked notion of a role model. Outside psychoanalytic contexts, what lies at the heart of the ways in which identification is used is the recognition of some sort of kinship, and giving this a positive value. I am using the idea of 'likeness' as a shorthand for these current, under-articulated assumptions. It is possible to take this likeness to be perfectly straightforward; in the examples I have cited it is construed in terms of race and gender. Governments, and those who work closely with them, have a strong investment in making these attributes simple in order to count them and use them as a means of judging 'social inclusion'. Yet the whole drift of scholarship over at least three decades has been to point out the formidable intricacy not just of the categories race, gender, and class, but religion, locality, nationality, and so on as well. 'The Black Heroes of Trafalgar' invited black readers (and others born outside the UK) to connect with Nelson's men, to feel elevated by their 'heroism', and to experience a direct link with the national festivities prompted by the bicentenary of his death.

Identification lies at the heart of historical practice and I would like to see it more widely discussed and understood. That its centrality is also implied in contemporary political and institutional practices makes its calm and thoughtful exploration all the more urgent. Mechanistic approaches, which offer audiences historical actors who are superficially the same as them, as if matching numbers in a game of dominoes, are more shallow than is intellectually or politically desirable. While these phenomena are general ones, they are brought into sharp relief by anniversaries, which are in fact predicated on finding and then cultivating the *current* connections with *past* events or figures. In the process, opportunities for shaping identifies are offered, as the 'Black Heroes' example reveals. A sense of connection, which is common to all the Nelson-related examples I have given, is further intensified by the specialness of an anniversary. Hence the idea that an interval of 200 years confers a heightened significance and grandeur on the occasion is present, but does not require constant emphasis, since it

---

[14] Ibid., p. 206.

draws on established conventions concerning the allure of round numbers. In this respect there is a subtle fit between popular culture and historical practice that frequently invokes decades, half-centuries, and centuries as organizing principles in need of no particular explanation or justification.

Non-specialists are amused by concepts such as 'the long eighteenth century', which challenges common sense, and signals on the one hand that business as usual involves ordinary centuries and on the other that here is a particular case that scholars need to reconceptualize.[15] For the most part, however, historians and others work more or less happily with round numbers; there has been a collective internalizing of their significance, although a moment's reflection reveals how arbitrary they are. Why should we push the boat out for a bicentenary, but not for an interval of 199, or indeed ninety-eight, forty-seven, or six years? Thus 'mere' conventions are involved, conventions that generate familiar labels and facilitate marketing. Furthermore, these labels are constantly being reinforced in our intimate lives through such events as birthdays and wedding anniversaries, and in our consuming lives through products that trade on commemoration, and hence need to offer easy recognition. Anniversaries and tags that facilitate audience recognition are now inseparable. Commemorative stamps neatly exemplify the point.

It will be clear that I wish to argue that there are dangers as well as opportunities in what we might call the commemoration industry, which is now a central aspect of history in public life. I adopt a critical stance precisely because public history is such an important phenomenon that all historians and institutions connected with history have no choice but to engage with issues that touch our professional lives, our scholarly values, our ethics. It is vital not to underestimate the ways in which a number of trends have become entwined. One of the most significant shifts of the last few decades has been the growth of both academic and popular interest in commemoration, memory, heritage, and their cognates. This development is closely related to, but hardly identical with, the belated engagement in Britain with public history, which had come into prominence considerably earlier in the United States, where it enjoys a notably high status.[16]

The shifts I have just mentioned are, I suspect, of different kinds. For example, the interest in memory derives, at least in part, from the marked increase in attention paid to psychoanalysis from the 1970s onwards. Although it remains a highly contentious field in many quarters, its status,

---

[15] For example, Frank O'Gorman, *The Long Eighteenth Century: British Political and Social History 1688–1832* (London, 1997).
[16] Jordanova, *History in Practice*, ch. 6.

breadth of influence, and the sheer volume of relevant publications have demonstrably grown. Some of the concern with anniversaries and commemoration, however, has been driven by responses to the Second World War as well as by enduring debates over the First. Phenomena such as the longevity of some survivors, many of whom are extraordinarily articulate, the desire on the part of governments and interest groups to build memorials, to speak about and assign guilt, and the widespread belief that visits to key sites—battlegrounds and concentration camps, for instance—will have a prophylactic effect, fuel what is indeed a commemoration *industry*. It is as if war and inhumanity are diseases that could be eliminated by a form of historical vaccination. The injections are the lessons learned from remembering the past. The fact that there is still unfinished business from the Great War, such as whether those shot for 'cowardice' were in fact suffering from shellshock and hence unjustly executed, allows that war to remain troublingly alive. Moreover, controversies about its historical interpretation are equally alive.[17] Similarly, in relation to the 1939–45 war, feelings about guilt and reparation are still raw. Marking key moments of those wars draws attention away from these complexities and offers forms of expression that are, albeit subtly, channelled. Marking times of war entails strategic simplification. Such anniversaries possess two distinct properties. On the one hand, they provide occasions suffused with decorum and ritual when thoughts and feelings may be expressed, while on the other, they remind people of the precise interval that has elapsed since the event in question. When there are survivors these activities possess special poignancy. In the course of public commemorative events, it is clear how many, or rather how few, are still alive, and the gradual decrease in their numbers becomes painfully visible.

The rise of public history in the United Kingdom, and elsewhere, is a distinct phenomenon in its own right, although the concomitant growth of curiosity about war in history, evident in the size of sections devoted to military history in bookshops, certainly plays its part. Public history builds on widespread enthusiasms for genealogy, for visiting 'heritage' sites, for treating museums as desirable venues for leisure activities. Its new prominence, manifest, for example, in conferences and dedicated courses in institutions of higher education, fits with changes in government policy, such as the drive to increase 'access' to culture, and with shifts within cultural institutions themselves, which have, of necessity, become more commercial. Many of those institutions are promoting history to as wide a public or

---

[17] For example Stephen Heathorn, 'The mnemonic turn in the cultural historiography of Britain's Great War', *The Historical Journal*, 48 (2005), 1103–24.

publics as possible. In this context anniversaries are special (marketing) opportunities.

Marking time happens all over the place. It shapes what goes under the name of 'history', hence the need for professional historians to engage with it in an informed manner. Smuggled into commemoration are assumptions about periodization, the nature of historical agency, causation, and the attribution of retrospective historical judgements. Such issues lie at the intellectual core of our discipline; accordingly there are compelling reasons for giving the constellation of phenomena around commemoration our critical attention. The fact that they lie at the intersection between an academic discipline and public life simply reinforces the point. However, there are a number of reasons why providing such critical attention is likely to prove challenging. Both historians and their field clearly benefit in some perfectly tangible ways from the trend towards ever greater commemorative heights. For example, the extraordinary celebrations that accompanied the bicentenary of (the beginning of) the French Revolution in 1989 provided publishing opportunities, publicity, exposure, and income that would not otherwise have been available. I am especially curious about what it really means not just to mark but to celebrate the 200th anniversary of a complex, emotive abstraction, the legacy of which is, and always has been, hotly contested. Perhaps it means no more than that, by tacit consent, 'the French Revolution' was commodified, turned into some*thing* that could be marketed. Since the French Revolution is frequently taken to mark the beginning of the modern world, its significance is hardly in doubt. In 1989 we were being invited to remember an event of world-historical importance.[18] The processes of remembering somehow had to deal with the vastly different responses the Revolution necessarily spawned. Ideally ways had to be found of judiciously weighing it up. Recasting the whole event as at once a celebration and a marketing opportunity does not neutralize but it does marginalize the political sting in the Revolution's tail. For me '1989' smacked of a kind of shameless opportunism, of a faintly indecent, greedy eagerness for attention. While there is no doubt that some important publications appeared in that year, and that the Revolution's significance was reaffirmed, it was achieved at a cost. Reification was one such cost—turning the Revolution into an event, rather than a messy array of overlapping processes given a single name for convenience.

The history of Bastille Day is pertinent here. On 14 July 1789, the Bastille Prison in Paris was stormed by a crowd who freed the small number of

[18] Simon Schama's *Citizens: A Chronicle of the French Revolution* (New York, 1989), one of the best-known books published in the bicentenary year, affirms, in its own distinctive way, the importance of the Revolution and of its multiple constituent narratives.

inmates in an act that became charged with symbolic significance. However, it was not given legal status as a national holiday until 1880, when the matter was hotly contested precisely because its celebration of republicanism constituted a specific reading of French history that monarchists, for example, could not accept. Its continued celebration is an important instance of the ways in which history, commemoration, and a sense of nationhood are yoked together in formidably complex ways. Late nineteenth- and early twentieth-century depictions show couples dancing in the streets, evocative images of pleasure and decorum—the men are behatted, for example. This is an annual event, and hence a type of anniversary quite distinct from the bicentenary of 1989. The partying element is certainly there, but so are the other two elements of celebration I identified earlier. In enacting the law of 1880, there was a quite precise intention to weigh up the significance of a past event and to give it its due. In the process, republicans were offered rich opportunities for identification with their political forebears. And in marking this event annually, a ritual emerged, with, for some at least, profound meaning, capable of being intensified at times of exceptional national significance. Hence the precise manner in which Bastille Day is marked continues to matter, and in this way, as indeed in many others, '1789' is a living presence in French life.[19]

On 22 October 2005, *The Scotsman* newspaper made 'commemoration' and 'celebration' its words of the week in recognition of the anniversary of the Battle of Trafalgar. The writer suggested that losers commemorate, since they can hardly celebrate—that is what the victors do. The article cited the definition of 'commemoration' in the *American Heritage Dictionary*—'the act of honouring the memory of or serving as a memorial to someone or something'.[20] Their distinction between celebration and commemoration is too simple. No one 'won' the French Revolution, which was both commemorated and celebrated. Furthermore there is no mention of what lies at the heart of anniversaries. Time has to elapse, and the precise amount of time has to be appropriate, even decorous. Anniversaries are all about intervals. The dictionary definition suggests that at any moment one might commemorate a thing or a person, whereas, when it comes to public history, this is clearly not the case. The vastness of the celebrations in 1989 corresponded to the size and roundness of the interval since the original event. The scale was apt for a 200-year interval;

---

[19] Rosemonde Sanson, *Les 14 juillet (1789–1975): Fête et conscience nationale* (Paris, 1976) and Jean-Pierre Bois, *Histoire des 14 juillet 1789–1919* (Rennes, 1991); both are illustrated, the latter more copiously, while documents relating to the 1880 law may be found in the former at pp. 202–8.

[20] George Kerevan, 'Word of the Week', *The Scotsman*, 22 October 2005.

that of Bastille Day is fitting for annual recognition.[21] It would be neither 'decent' nor feasible to have another extravaganza before a further substantial interval had elapsed, yet an annual day on its own distinctive scale works. Thus the interval matters, and not only in practical terms; its length shapes both the content and the spirit of anniversary celebrations. The conventionalized spaces between anniversaries form an important component of the ritualized acts of remembrance that they constitute.

However, the dictionary definition introduces a major concept into these discussions, one that is exceptionally hard for contemporary historical practice to deal with. I refer to the idea of honouring. In concluding the essay, I would like to consider briefly this emotionally and morally charged notion. At first sight it seems plausible that many forms of memory and of commemorative practices are linked together through honouring. In celebrating the 200th anniversary of Nelson's death, we acknowledge and pay tribute to him and his achievements. Yet we also weigh them up, with the result that aspects of him that were, quite literally, *dis*honourable need to be considered. We manage the resulting complexities by pointing out that his faults make him more 'human'. Accordingly, it becomes possible to say, as Lucy Moore does in *Great Britons*, 'in his very weaknesses lay Nelson's strengths'. In this formulation, we honour him, having weighed up the full range of his attributes, both 'good' and 'bad'. Yet this is a fragile position, certainly secured by the interval that has elapsed since his death, and possibly in addition by shifts in moral values—for example, Horatio and Emma's profound and passionate love becomes self-justifying.[22] In honouring we generally experience the need for careful adjudication, lest the object of respect reveal a fault that makes those paying homage uncertain of its worth and perhaps also of their own values.

Honouring *individuals* is part of the fabric of our lives; it entails just those processes of identification, which, as I noted earlier, inform both public history and government policies. Honouring a putative *event* such as the French Revolution is considerably more problematic; it stretches the common-sense understanding of the term. It only makes sense if recast as a special form of recognition that involves assessment, an elaborate operation that weighs up a legacy, embraces historical complexity. Here, then, is the heart of the challenge that anniversaries and related phenomena pose to professional historians. We are obligated to evaluate and judge. The com-

---

[21] A comparison with Armistice Day might be fruitful: see Adrian Gregory, *The Silence of Memory: Armistice Day 1919–1946* (Oxford and Providence, RI, 1994).

[22] Cooper, *Great Britons*, p. 84. On p. 85, a still from the 1941 film *Lady Hamilton* is reproduced. It depicts an intimate moment between Emma and Horatio as played, with manifest erotic charge, by Vivien Leigh and Laurence Olivier.

memoration industry works to simplify, commodify, and package the past. In the process, it invokes emotionally charged subjects, such as memory and remembrance. Subject to complex forces of necessity, this industry mobilizes only some aspects of celebration, it selects only part of honouring. When it invites historians in, it generally does so on its own terms. Inevitably these offers are tempting and they are often couched in languages historians think they can and must do business with. Naturally, each case, each anniversary must be judged on its merits. Nonetheless there are general patterns, patterns that bear upon the contemporary practice of history as a discipline, which it is useful to note. In my essay I have resisted the idea that a passionate commitment to public history involves uncritical participation in anniversary phenomena. On the contrary, that commitment enjoins us to set our own terms and standards, to be fearless both in looking the past in the face and re-presenting it to wide audiences—frank appraisal is arguably the most profound and enduring form of tribute yet developed.

Dedication. I dedicate this essay to the memory of a beloved friend, Patricia Peacock, who died during its composition and whose life and death bear directly on the themes I explore. She was born on 11 September 1924; we celebrated her birthday together in 2001—an exceptionally sharp sense of anniversaries was forged as a result. Her account of finding, only relatively recently, the grave of her brother, a pilot shot down in France during the Second World War, has prompted me to keep thinking about, for want of a better word, remembrance. The service held after her death was truly celebratory of a life lived with exceptional compassion and generosity. I had already written the passage on celebration and death and have decided not to change it. Nonetheless I wanted to honour, to express my appreciation for the life of a person, who in dying and death, as in life, gave others the chance to celebrate.

Note. I thank Kenneth Fincham and Holger Hoock for their kindness in reading drafts and offering constructive help, Karl Figlio for advice on 'identification', and participants at the conference in January 2006 for their stimulating papers and comments.

I
1805–1905

2.

'His dirge our groans—his monument our praise': Official and Popular Commemoration of Nelson in 1805–6

COLIN WHITE

Introduction

On 7 December 1805 the King's Theatre in London staged a new drama, *Naval Victory and Triumph of Lord Nelson*. A month earlier, the news had reached Britain of the victory at the Battle of Trafalgar on 21 October and the death of the British commander-in-chief, Vice Admiral Lord Nelson and, since then, theatres had been vying with each other to mount ever more ambitious and spectacular commemorative pieces. At first, all went well: the opening scene, depicting the battle itself, was greeted with rapturous applause. But then, as *The Times* reported, came a scene depicting Nelson 'in the cabin of the *Victory* in the convulsions of his last moments'. At this, the theatre erupted with cries of 'Off! Off!' and even when the singer and author John Braham stepped onto the stage to assure the angry audience that if any scene was objectionable it would be removed, his offer was greeted with cries of 'All! All!', especially from the Pit—in other words, the cheaper seats. Clearly, Braham and his associates had badly misjudged the public mood: as *The Times* commented, 'The scene was too strong for the feelings of those who loved and admired [Nelson].'[1]

Accounts of the public reaction to the news of Trafalgar and the death of Nelson tend to depict a general, and unified, national mood of sorrow and loss. This trend was begun by the Poet Laureate, Robert Southey, who wrote in the famous peroration to his *Life of Nelson*, published in 1813, 'The death of Nelson was felt in England as something more than a public calamity: men started at the intelligence and turned pale as if they had heard of the loss of a dear friend.' And it has continued to the present—as

[1] *The Times*, 9 December 1805.

23

one of Nelson's most recent biographers, Andrew Lambert, puts it, 'The public reaction to Nelson's death was universal, as numerous writers have testified.'[2] But Braham's barracking by the King's Theatre audience is a striking reminder that in fact the national mood in 1805–6 was rather more nuanced than the older accounts suggest. For example, the people who angrily protested at the portrayal of Nelson's death on stage were, at the same time, eagerly demanding, and buying, inexpensive paintings on glass or ceramics depicting the death scene, and reading rival newspaper accounts of the hero's final moments which gave conflicting versions of his last words. Moreover, the suggestion that the King's Theatre protest was led by the people in the cheaper seats in the house is significant: as we shall see, there is evidence that the responses of the social and political elite to Nelson's death, especially in art, were regarded as excessive, or even inappropriate, by members of the commercial and working classes. Repeatedly, the official accounts and depictions of Nelson's death, and the reactions to it—even the elaborate funeral ceremonies staged in London in early January 1806—were challenged in popular ballads and caricatures. It is clear that there was an undercurrent of unease with some of the more elaborate and contrived expressions of grief.

This essay will examine and analyse the many ways in which Nelson's death was commemorated in 1805–6. It will also highlight contemporary commentary on those commemorations. What emerges is a more subtly balanced view of the national mourning.

The News Breaks

At about one o'clock in the morning of 6 November 1805, the Secretary to the Board of Admiralty, William Marsden, had just finished a long day's work in the Board Room and was making his way to his apartments. Suddenly, he was confronted with a middle-aged man, in the uniform of a lieutenant, whose dishevelled appearance showed that he had just completed a long and arduous journey. As Marsden later remembered, 'In accosting me, the officer used these impressive words, "Sir, we have gained a great victory; but we have lost Lord Nelson!" '[3]

Lieutenant John Lapenotiere had spent thirty-seven hours in a post-chaise on the road from Falmouth, following a nine-day voyage in the small

---

[2] Robert Southey, *The Life of Nelson* (London, 1813), vol. 2, pp. 272–3; Andrew Lambert, *Britannia's God of War* (London, 2004), p. 312.
[3] William Marsden, *A Brief Memoir of the Life and Writings of William Marsden* (London, 1838), p. 116.

schooner HMS *Pickle* through gale-swept seas. He brought with him the first news of the Battle of Trafalgar, contained in a long dispatch written by Vice Admiral Cuthbert Collingwood, who had succeeded to the command of the British fleet following the death of Nelson.[4]

At once, the government's efficient communications machinery was set in motion. Having roused and briefed the First Lord, Lord Barham, Marsden dispatched messengers to the King at Windsor, Prime Minister William Pitt, and the Lord Mayor of London. In the meantime a team of clerks was collected together and copies of the dispatch were made for the newspapers. By late afternoon, a special edition of the *London Gazette* was available, while 3,000 copies had been sent to Great Yarmouth, there to be loaded on a fast packet-boat to carry the news to the Continent.

Everywhere, the reactions echoed the mixed message of Lapenotiere's first excited words to Marsden—elation at the victory was tempered by sorrow at Nelson's death. 'We do not know whether we should mourn or rejoice,' commented *The Times*. 'The country has gained the most splendid and decisive Victory that has ever graced the naval annals of England; but it has been dearly purchased. The great and gallant NELSON is no more.' When Lady Elizabeth Foster went to the Admiralty for more news, she found, 'every countenance was dejected—nor could one have guessed that it was a victory with 20 ships of the line taken from the enemy, only that defeat would have caused tumult and this was the silence of sorrow and respect.' Marsden himself later remembered that he had been 'oppressed with the contradictory feelings of triumph for the country and sorrow for the loss of the greatest hero we ever had'.[5]

When Parliament met in late January 1806, the customary addresses were moved to congratulate the king on the victory. Here, too, the mood was as much of sorrow as of celebration. Speaking in the House of Lords, the Earl of Essex said, 'Great as the victory of Trafalgar was, the universal sorrow with which the intelligence of the heroic Commander who fell in it was received by the Country proved that the triumph of that day had not been cheaply purchased.'[6] Many were inspired to write poetry, including George Canning, then Treasurer to the Navy, who had accompanied Nelson as he pushed through the cheering crowds in Portsmouth on his

[4] For the best account of Lapenotiere's voyage, based on the latest research, see Derek Allen and Peter Hore, *News of Nelson* (London, 2005).

[5] *The Times*, 7 November 1805; Lady Elizabeth Foster: Lord Granville Leveson Gower, *Private Correspondence, 1781–1821* (London, 1916), vol. 2, p. 112; Marsden, *Brief Memoir*, p. 118.

[6] Nicholas Harris Nicolas, *The Dispatches and Letters of Vice Admiral Lord Nelson KB*, 7 vols (London, 1845–6), vol. 7, p. 315.

last walk on English soil on 14 September. His poem, 'Ulm and Trafalgar', published in early 1806, included the passage:

> O price his conquering Country grieved to pay
> O dear-bought glories of Trafalgar's day!
> Lamented hero! When to Britain's shore
> Exulting fame those aweful tidings bore
> Joy's bursting shout in whelming grief was drowned
> And Victory's self unwilling audience found;
> On every brow the cloud of sadness hung
> The sounds of triumph died on every tongue![7]

Nor were such sentiments confined to the social and political elite. At Aylsham, in Norfolk, there was a procession to the church featuring over twenty banners, each bearing an appropriate legend, including: 'We rejoice for our Country, but mourn for our Friend' and 'Almighty God has blessed His Majesty's arms', the latter a quotation from Nelson's dispatch reporting his victory at the Battle of the Nile in August 1798. In Cornwall, the militia paraded and fired a salute in celebration—but they were all wearing black armbands with 'Nelson immortalised' inscribed on them.[8]

As soon as the news of Trafalgar began to spread, the London theatres began to mount increasingly spectacular tributes—and all of them commented on Nelson's death. On the evening of 6 November the Theatre Royal, Drury Lane, presented a brief interlude featuring 'Rule Britannia' and some hurriedly written verses lamenting Nelson: 'His dirge our groans—his monument our praise.' But at Covent Garden the management was even more enterprising. After the last play of the evening, the audience were treated to 'a view of the English fleet riding triumphantly' while a group of naval officers were discovered 'in attitudes of admiration'. As they gazed heavenwards, a medallion was lowered bearing a portrait of Nelson surrounded by rays of glory. The whole company then led the audience in singing 'Rule Britannia', including a new verse written specially for the occasion which ended:

> Rule, brave Britons, rule the main,
> Avenge the god-like hero slain!

Not to be outdone, Drury Lane responded the next night with a short sketch, mounted with still more impressive scenic effects. This time it was the figure of Fame who descended from the skies, carrying the first of many

---

[7] Nicolas, *Dispatches*, vol. 7, p. 357.
[8] *The Times*, 10 November 1805.

misquotations of Nelson's Trafalgar signal, 'England expects everyone will do his duty.'[9]

Such theatricality extended even to the Lord Mayor's Banquet in the London Guildhall on 9 November, when Prime Minister William Pitt made his ringing claim, 'England has saved herself by her exertions; and will, as I trust, save Europe by her example.'[10] The mayor and his chief guest sat under an illuminated arch bearing the words 'Nelson and Victory'; behind them hung a portrait of Nelson. Also on display were a sword and the legend: 'The sword of the French Admiral Blanquet, the gift of Lord Nelson to the City of London in the year 1798'.

A month later, on Tuesday 5 December, the whole nation observed a Day of Thanksgiving for the victory. The tone was set by a special collect written for the occasion: 'Let not Thy gracious goodness towards us, in the signal Victory which Thou hast given us over the common Enemy, be frustrated by a presumptuous confidence in our own might,' and throughout the land bishops, priests, and ministers improved on this theme. The Revd Thomas Wood, preaching at a service at which a collection was taken for the Patriotic Fund, set up by Lloyds for the relief of the wounded and the dependents of those killed, concentrated mostly on Nelson: 'His Name is a monument that will exist undiminished throughout all ages and be warmly cherished in the remembrance of Britons.' At the Salter's Hall, the Revd Hugh Worthington unknowingly echoed Nelson's own pre-battle prayer, when he warned: 'Let there be no malignity against the enemies with which we contend.'[11]

The public mood also manifested itself in a voracious demand for commemorative material. Prints, ceramics, glassware, jewellery, enamel boxes, textiles, and even furniture were hurriedly mass-produced—all with a mourning theme. Two images predominated. First, there was the Death of Nelson—usually depicted with very little attempt at historical accuracy—and, second, there were allegorical depictions of the national mourning—usually involving Britannia and/or sailors standing beside the hero's tomb/ashes. Even Nelson's mistress, Emma, Lady Hamilton, took part, appearing in a popular print by Thomas Baxter showing Britannia crowning the bust of the hero with laurel (Figure 2.1). The intensity of the demand, and the resulting frenzy of commercial activity, can be seen in all the surviving collections of Nelsonia. For example, more than 25 per cent of the Lily Lambert McCarthy Collection of Nelson memorabilia at the

---

[9] *The Times*, 12 November 1805.
[10] Quoted in William Hague, *William Pitt the Younger* (London, 2004), p. 565.
[11] All the material for this paragraph was located in the Michael Nash Archive. I am indebted to Mr Nash for allowing me access to his fascinating private collection.

Royal Naval Museum has a 'death' or 'mourning' theme.[12] Similarly, a recent definitive study of the primitive paintings on glass produced for the cheaper end of the market has shown that well over half of the surviving Nelson-related examples depict his death.[13]

The expression of official and popular grief was therefore both widespread and voluminous. Even so, occasional hints of unease do emerge. The 7 December protest in the King's Theatre was echoed in a caricature by Charles Williams, also dating from December 1805, which sounds a cautionary note about the excessive public expressions of grief (Figure 2.2). Jack, a sailor home from the battle, is being greeted by his girlfriend Poll at Portsmouth. She, all swooning sensibility, her eyes cast devoutly upwards to heaven, is trying to comfort him: 'Welcome! welcome home my Dear Jack!! Ah! but you have not brought the brave Lord Nelson with you, well I hope he is in Heaven.' But Jack, his face grimly set, has no time for such histrionics. 'In Heaven!' he exclaims, rummaging in his snuffbox, 'aye to be sure he is Poll—what in H__ should prevent him.'

The State Funeral

Meanwhile Nelson's body was being brought home on board HMS *Victory*, carefully preserved in a barrel of brandy. After calling briefly at Portsmouth on 4–5 December, the battered flagship was ordered round to the Nore, the great anchorage at the mouth of the Thames. There she was met by the *Chatham*, the official yacht of the Commissioner of Chatham Royal Dockyard. She was bearing a curious cargo. Six years before, in the Mediterranean, one of Nelson's captains, Ben Hallowell, had presented him with a simple plain coffin, made of wood taken from the wreckage of *L'Orient*, the French flagship at the Battle of the Nile, which had caught fire and blown up at the height of the action. It suited Nelson's slightly macabre sense of humour and he had carefully preserved it. Now he was to be laid to rest in it, as Hallowell had intended.[14]

On 22 December, the body was finally transferred from the *Victory* to the *Chatham* and taken upriver to the Naval Hospital at Greenwich—the famous institution for sick and wounded sailors on the banks of the River Thames. There, the plain trophy coffin and its leaden shell were encased in a magnificent casket specially designed by the Ackerman brothers. Covered

---

[12] Lily McCarthy, *Remembering Nelson* (Portsmouth, 1995).

[13] Leslie LeQuesne, *Nelson Commemorated in Glass Pictures* (Woodbridge, 2001).

[14] Unless otherwise stated, the following description of the state funeral is taken from the *Naval Chronicle* 15 (January–June 1806), 1–75.

Figure 2.1. Thomas Baxter, *Britannia Crowning the Bust of the Hero with Laurel*, coloured engraving (1805). Emma Hamilton in her favourite role—a print produced shortly after the news of Trafalgar arrived in Britain in 1805. © National Maritime Museum.

Figure 2.2. Charles Williams, *Jack and Poll at Portsmouth*, engraving (1805). The blunt sailor questions the excessive public expressions of grief at Nelson's death. © National Maritime Museum.

in gilded heraldic devices and other symbolic decorations, such as crocodiles (another allusion to the Battle of the Nile) and seahorses, it was so impressive that the organizers of the lying-in-state left it displayed to the public gaze, instead of covering it with a black pall as custom would have required.

Custom was to play a large part in the ceremonial that followed. It was one of the last full heraldic funerals ever staged in Britain and all the details were in the hands of the College of Arms, under Garter King of Arms, Sir Isaac Heard. The coffin was accompanied throughout its long journey by the hero's helmet, surcoat, shield, and gauntlets. Of course none of these had actually been worn by Nelson: they were all specially made for the occasion. It was almost as if a medieval knight was going to his rest, an analogy made at the time by the Chaplain of the *Victory*, the Revd Alexander Scott, who insisted on remaining with his patron and friend until the last moment. Writing to Emma Hamilton from his vigil beside Nelson's body, Scott said, 'So help me God as I think he was a true knight and worthy the age of chivalry.'[15]

The story of the state funeral has been retold in successive biographies and the full account can be found in a number of contemporary publications, most notably the *Naval Chronicle*, which devoted some fifty pages to a precise description of the event. All these re-creations give an impression of a spectacle that was both smooth-running and enormously impressive—a view supported by the superb prints produced by artists such as Daniel Orme.[16] But they are all based on the official orders and so describe what *ought* to have happened, rather than what actually occurred on the day—a fact spotted by one of the onlookers in the huge crowd attending the ceremonies, John Williams, writing to his father in Anglesey: 'How can you believe a word in the Papers as to our military operations at a distance when I tell you that they all differ in their accounts of the Regts which passed under their own windows—and all wrong.'[17]

Recent research has shown that underlying the apparently flawless ceremonial there were a number of last-minute changes of plan—some of them imposed on the unwilling organizers by popular pressure.[18] When

[15] Thomas Pettigrew, *Memoirs of the Life of Vice-Admiral Lord Nelson* (London, 1849), vol. 2, p. 553.
[16] Francis Blagdon, *Orme's Graphic History of the Life, Exploits and Death of Horatio Viscount Nelson* (London, 1806).
[17] Royal Naval Museum, Portsmouth (RNM): RNM 56/9.
[18] Colin White, 'The Immortal Memory: the development of the Nelson Legend from 1805 to the present', in Colin White (ed.), *The Nelson Companion* (Stroud, 1995), pp. 1–31; Timothy Jenks, 'Contesting the hero: the funeral of Admiral Lord Nelson', *Journal of British Studies*, 39 (2000), 22–53; Marianne Czisnik, *Horatio Nelson: A Controversial Hero* (London, 2005).

the initial proposals for the processions were published, the newspapers spotted that there was no mention of the sailors of HMS *Victory* and a vigorous press campaign began for them to be included. Eventually, they were allowed to carry the shot-torn colours of their ship—and they completely stole the show. Similarly, when he noticed that the *Victory*'s Royal Marines were missing in the first set of official orders, the Adjutant General, Royal Marines, Lieutenant-General John Campbell, wrote to William Marsden on 31 December: 'I beg leave to suggest to their Lordships that the Chatham Division from the Artillery Companies and a selection of the *Victory*'s detachment, can furnish a Guard not exceeding 100 men which for discipline and appearance will not discredit any procession.'[19] He got his way.

There were also squabbles over who should attend, and of course, as always on such occasions, precedence was much disputed. The Prince of Wales originally indicated his intention of attending in his official capacity but the King forbade it, so he said he would take part as a private citizen. Even this gave rise to controversy, for the Lord Mayor of London then claimed precedence over him within the City boundaries.[20] Heard received a tetchy letter from Lord Hood, Governor of Greenwich Hospital: 'I do not comprehend what you say, that you *apprehend* I shall be one of the Chief Mourners; why not say that I am to be one as the arrangements *solely* rest with you.'[21] On 6 January Nelson's elder brother William, newly ennobled as Earl Nelson, wrote to deny a rumour that his brother had asked his chaplain, the Revd Alexander Scott, to perform the burial service: 'I think it my duty to give [you] this information in order to satisfy yourself, as well as the Bishop of London, who I am told has not been quite pleased with the other report.'[22]

As the admiral's senior male relative, Earl Nelson might have expected to play the role of Chief Mourner at the funeral, but the College of Arms decided instead to give that role to the Navy's senior admiral—the Admiral of the Fleet, Sir Peter Parker—thus symbolizing the Navy's importance to the state.[23] The gesture also emphasized the continuity of naval service, for by a happy coincidence, Parker had been one of Nelson's earliest patrons and had helped engineer some of Nelson's key career movements—including the all-important promotion to post captain in 1779. Similarly, the key

---

[19] National Archives, ADM1/3246.
[20] Jenks, 'Contesting the hero', 29.
[21] RNM 92/240 (2).
[22] RNM 92/240 (1).
[23] For a fuller examination of this aspect of the funeral see Holger Hoock, 'Nelson entombed: the military and naval pantheon in St Paul's Cathedral', in David Cannadine (ed.), *Admiral Lord Nelson: Context and Legacy* (London, 2005), pp. 115–43, at 116.

roles in the heraldic elements of the ceremony (normally, at the funeral of a landowning nobleman, played by the tenants of the deceased) were, in this case, given to naval officers. For example, the 'Banner of Emblems', symbolizing the nation's grief, was carried by Captain Thomas Hardy of the *Victory*; the pall-bearers were all admirals, as were the supporters of the canopy, and Nelson's banner as a Knight of the Order of the Bath was carried by Captain Richard Moorsom, who had commanded the battleship *Revenge* at Trafalgar. As Nelson went to his rest, he was surrounded by men who had known him well and who represented every stage of his long naval career (Figure 2.3).

The ceremonies were spread over five days between 5 and 9 January 1806. First, the body lay in state for three days in the Painted Hall at Greenwich Hospital. Black hangings covered the vivid wall paintings that gave the hall its name; brightly coloured heraldic devices gleamed in the rich glow from hundreds of candles in special wall sconces. And arranged round the body, in its richly decorated coffin, were captured French and Spanish flags.

On Wednesday 8 January, there was a 'Grand River Procession' from Greenwich to London. A large flotilla was assembled, with many smaller craft escorting sixteen principal barges. Among these were the State Barge of the City of London, a magnificent, gilded vessel, and eleven barges owned by the City Livery Companies, their colourful banners snapping in the wind. The coffin was placed in one of the royal barges, originally made for Charles II and now, appropriately, rowed by sailors from the *Victory*. Its bright gilding and paint had been shrouded in black velvet, and a large canopy, surmounted by black feathers, erected over the stern. It became a treasured Nelson relic, and is now displayed in the Royal Naval Museum, alongside the *Victory*, in Portsmouth.

Slowly the long line advanced upriver towards London, its passage marked by the dull thuds and white puffs of smoke from the minute guns, fired from small gunboats stationed along the route. The weather was fine, and the ceremony had been timed so that the procession had the flood tide flowing under it. But a strong wind was blowing from the south-west, setting up a heavy chop on the river, and the oarsmen had a constant struggle to keep the unwieldy barges on station. The Thames had been closed to traffic and, in places, the hundreds of trading vessels that usually used the river were stacked three or four deep, their masts and yards crowded with spectators. Meanwhile thousands more were watching from the shore, pushing down to the water's edge for a better view.

After passing through the Pool of London, where the crowds were even larger, the procession eventually arrived at Whitehall Stairs, near Westminster. There, the coffin was unloaded and taken to the Admiralty.

THE CEREMONY OF LORD NELSON'S INTERMENT IN S.^T PAULS CATHEDRAL, JAN.^Y 9TH 1806.

Figure 2.3. *The Ceremony of Lord Nelson's Interment in St Paul's Cathedral.* Daniel Orme's detailed depiction of the final moments of the service in St Paul's, in January 1806, just before the coffin was lowered into the crypt. Aquatint & etching (1806). © National Maritime Museum.

As the barge came alongside the stairs, the sky suddenly darkened and a squall of wind and rain erupted, soaking and buffeting the bearers as they struggled with the heavy coffin.

The following day, 9 January, the coffin was placed on a massive funeral car, designed to look like the *Victory*. It was escorted by a long procession made up mainly of soldiers. The only naval contingents were pensioners from Greenwich Hospital and the members of the *Victory*'s crew, who proudly carried their ship's enormous battle ensigns, opening them up from time to time to display the shot holes to the admiring crowd. Finally the body arrived at St Paul's Cathedral, where every nearby building was packed with spectators and a special stand had been erected above the great west portico. Inside, the cathedral had been transformed into a huge amphitheatre by the erection of more stands in the nave and underneath the great dome, accommodating a congregation of some 7,000. By now the short January afternoon was drawing to its close: a special lantern, mounted with 130 individual lamps, had been suspended from the dome.

The service that followed was striking both for simplicity and for highly charged emotion. It had been decided that the Burial Service would be performed within the context of Evensong, said or sung daily, then as now, in churches and cathedrals throughout the land. Nelson, the Norfolk parson's son, was sent to his rest with the ringing words of the Book of Common Prayer, familiar to him since early boyhood—so familiar indeed, that his own fine prayers often echo the language and cadences of Thomas Cranmer. The music was a special selection of choral pieces by various English composers, put together by John Page, one of the St Paul's Vicars Choral. The choir, of about 100 boys and men from St Paul's, Westminster Abbey, the Chapel Royal, and St George's Chapel, Windsor, was conducted by the Revd John Pridden, one of the St Paul's Minor Canons. The organ was played by Thomas Attwood, who also composed a 'Grand Funeral Dirge'.[24]

The service began with the singing of William Croft's haunting setting of the Burial Sentences from the Book of Common Prayer, as the coffin was carried up the long nave. Following it, among all the naval officers, were the male members of Nelson's family, including his sixteen-year-old nephew George Matcham, who recorded in his diary, 'it was the most aweful sight I ever saw'.[25] At the climax of the service, the coffin was carried into the huge

---

[24] This description of the music is based on a printed copy of the original sheet music in the collection of the Royal Naval Museum. The full service was reconstructed by Colin White, using this material, and performed by Portsmouth Cathedral Choir in 1999. It has been recorded by Herald: HAVPCD232.

[25] Tom Pocock, *Trafalgar* (London, 2005), p. 210.

space underneath the dome and set high on a catafalque for all to see. The last words were read: the powerful phrases of the Committal, 'earth to earth; ashes to ashes; dust to dust'. The last anthem was sung: a special arrangement of one of Handel's great choruses, 'His body is buried in peace—but his name liveth evermore!' Then the coffin began to sink slowly from sight into the crypt below. As it disappeared, a signal was sent to Moorfields, where the troops who had escorted the body in the great procession had been drawn up. The artillery fired off a salute and the infantry fired three volleys into the air. As the gunfire reverberated around London, Sir Isaac Heard read out the full titles of the deceased; then the officers of Nelson's Household broke their white staves of office across their knees and handed them to Heard to be thrown into the grave.

At this point, the official rubric required that the *Victory's* sailors should reverently fold up the shot-torn colours and place them on a convenient table. But in a moment of spontaneity, which sent a frisson of emotion around the spectators beneath the dome, the sailors first ripped off a large portion of one of the flags and then subdivided it into smaller portions to be kept as mementoes. Watching from one of the stands, Mrs Codrington, whose husband had commanded the *Orion* at Trafalgar, commented: 'That was *Nelson*—the rest was so much the Herald's Office.'[26] It was a shrewd observation. Amidst all the melancholy splendour of the stately ceremonies, the sailors had remained true to the unique, maverick spirit of their great commander.

The unorthodox behaviour of the sailors was matched by that of the huge crowds that watched each stage of the spectacle. It is clear from the contemporary accounts that, before the event, members of the social and political elite were acutely uneasy about the presence of what they almost unanimously referred to as 'the mob'—and were considerably surprised to find them so calm and well-behaved. Lady Bessborough, who watched the street procession from a window recalled, 'Among the many touching things the silence of that immense Mob was not the least striking.' There were some violent scenes at Greenwich, when the volume of people queuing to see the lying-in-state led to scuffles and even to injuries, and the Governor of the Hospital, Lord Hood, was so alarmed that he called out the militia. There was no repetition of such scenes on subsequent days— but there was a certain amount of what might be termed 'audience participation'. The *Victory's* sailors were 'repeatedly and almost continually cheered' as they proudly carried their ship's colours through the streets. When the superbly decorated coffin was brought out of the Admiralty and

---

[26] Pocock, *Trafalgar*, p. 208.

placed on the elaborate hearse for the journey to St Paul's, the crowd in the immediate vicinity demanded that it should be left exposed to view, rather than being covered with the pall, as the official orders required. At times, the crowd briefly became active participants in the proceedings, as Lady Bessborough remembered: 'the moment the [funeral] Car appear'd which bore the body you might have heard a pin fall, and without any order to do so they all took off their hats. I cannot tell you the effect this simple action produc'd; it seemed one general impulse of respect beyond anything that could have been said or contrived.' The young Frederick Marryat, who was in the crowd with his father, recalled that the removal of the hats made a noise like the rushing of the waves on the seashore.[27]

Popular interest in the funeral extended well beyond the streets of London. The day of the funeral was marked elsewhere in Britain with the tolling of bells and with parades and assemblies. In Bristol, for example, the band of the North Gloucestershire Militia performed a solemn dirge. A replica of the coffin was displayed in Lincoln's Assembly Rooms. Hull went one stage further and reproduced the entire lying-in-state. Provincial theatres staged re-enactments of the street procession; a concert of the funeral music was performed at the Foundling Hospital, and the music itself was collected together and published in a special edition.[28] Crowds also queued at St Paul's to see the grave, which was left open with the coffin still visible, while, in an attempt to win back the tourists, Westminster Abbey commissioned a special wax effigy of Nelson from the artist Catherine Andras and obtained some of the admiral's own clothes in which to dress it.[29] Again, some evidence survives of unease at the extent of this hero-worship. When the Dean and Chapter of St Paul's tried to capitalize on Nelson's popularity by introducing an entrance fee to see the grave, there was public outcry. A popular ballad, speaking for Nelson, lamented:

> A mercenary crew
> Expose my lonely tomb to view
> And by the thirst of gain misled
> Invade the quiet of the dead.[30]

And in a vivid caricature entitled *The Sailor's Monument*, William Holland depicted a disgruntled sailor standing, arms folded, in front of his private monument to Nelson, made up of his sea chest, two rum barrels, two swords and a cocked hat, set up under a willow tree hung with black crepe

---

[27] Lady Bessborough: Gower, *Private Correspondence*, vol. 2, p. 145; Marryat: Christopher Lloyd, *Captain Marryat and the Old Navy* (London, 1939), p. 2.
[28] Czisnik, *Horatio Nelson*, p. 13.
[29] Richard Walker, *The Nelson Portraits* (Portsmouth, 1998), pp. 170–5.
[30] Quoted in Hoock, 'Nelson entombed', p. 133.

(Figure 2.4). 'I'll be no Twopenny Customer at St Paul's,' he says stubbornly; and, 'This shall be poor Jack's Monument, in his little Garden, to his Noble Companion.'[31]

The 'Heroification' of Nelson

Reporting the funeral, the *Naval Chronicle* proclaimed proudly, 'Thus terminated one of the most impressive and most splendid solemnities that ever took place in this Country, or perhaps Europe.' There had, of course, been others much more splendid; but few could have matched Nelson's state funeral in symbolic significance. For it was in a very real sense an apotheosis, marking the moment when he passed from mortal man to immortal hero.

The study of Nelson in his 'heroic' incarnation, as a cultural phenomenon rather than purely as a military leader, is a comparatively new scholarly development. The process began with the publication in 1995 of *The Nelson Companion*, a collection of essays by leading Nelson historians, looking at various aspects of the Nelson story. It was in this book that the phrase now in general use, 'the Nelson Legend', was first coined. A number of individual essays and monographs followed, including Timothy Jenks's seminal review of the state funeral.[32] In 2004, the Institute of Historical Research and the National Maritime Museum jointly organized the lecture series 'Rediscovering Nelson', published later as *Admiral Lord Nelson: Context and Legacy*.[33] That year also saw the publication of Andrew Lambert's biography *Nelson: Britannia's God of War*, rather more than a third of which deals with Nelson's heroic 'afterlife'. Finally, in 2005, Marianne Czisnik published her important examination of the Legend, *Horatio Nelson: A Controversial Hero*. As a result of all this new work, we now understand much better the process by which Nelson was transformed into The Hero—a process that began in the months immediately following his death.

It can be seen, for example, in the way in which the details of Nelson's death were reported. As soon as the news reached Britain, newspapers vied with each other to tell the story of Trafalgar, leading in each case with the death of Nelson; some very inaccurate accounts circulated. *The Times* reported that his last words had been, 'I know I am dying. I wish I could

---

[31] Quoted in Matthew Sheldon, 'A survey of Nelson's appearance in caricature', *The Trafalgar Chronicle*, 14 (2004), 1–10, at 7.
[32] Jenks, 'Contesting the hero'.
[33] Cannadine (ed.), *Admiral Lord Nelson*.

Figure 2.4. *The Sailor's Monument—to the Memory of Lord Nelson.* William Holland's disgruntled sailor protests at the imposition of charges to view Nelson's tomb in St Paul's Cathedral. Coloured etching (1805). © National Maritime Museum.

have survived to breathe my last upon British ground, but God's will be done.'[34] The *Gibraltar Chronicle* was even more imaginative: 'During the heat of the action His Lordship was severely wounded in the side and was obliged to be carried below. Immediately on his wound being dressed he insisted on being brought upon deck when shortly afterwards he received a shot through his body.'[35] Gradually, however, accounts began to emerge that were based on eyewitness accounts. First into print was the *Victory's* purser, Walter Burke, whose brief account was published in *The Morning Chronicle* in December[36] and included the first version of Nelson's actual last words, 'I have done my duty, I praise God for it.' Burke also mentioned the famous request for a kiss from Hardy. Around the same time, the ship's chaplain, Alexander Scott, wrote an account for Nelson's friend George Rose, the Vice-President of the Board of Trade, which was circulated privately.[37] Then, on 28 December, the *Chronicle* printed another, and more detailed, account, this time the joint work of Burke and William Beatty, the *Victory's* Surgeon. This aroused so much interest that Beatty went on to prepare his famous *Authentic Narrative of the Death of Lord Nelson*, published in early 1807.[38] Quickly established as the 'authorized version' of Nelson's death, every account since of the famous scene in the *Victory's* cockpit has relied heavily upon it. It purports to be an exact, blow-by-blow account of the event, with every broken phrase and sentence recorded, and pervaded throughout by a mood of sombre reflection, so that it reads almost like a Passion narrative from one of the Gospels. However, recent textual analysis, by Brockliss, Cardwell, and Moss, has demonstrated convincingly that it is a 'construct' made up from a number of different accounts and considerably tidied up:

> This is not to say that Beatty invented the *Authentic Narrative*. It is reasonable to assume that his story is largely chronologically accurate. What he did was to turn a series of sketches into a play. . . . [H]e took the liberty of embellishing half-remembered snatches of dialogue so that readers would be given an account of Nelson's death which would make sense of the conflicting reports and gel with the received image of the hero.[39]

A similar process occurred in the way that Nelson's death was portrayed by artists. The earliest depictions showed him still on deck, sometimes even

---

[34] *The Times*, 7 November 1805.
[35] *Gibraltar Chronicle*, 28 October 1805.
[36] *The Morning Chronicle*, 10 December 1805.
[37] Nicolas, *Dispatches*, vol. 7, p. 246.
[38] William Beatty, *The Authentic Narrative of the Death of Lord Nelson* (London 1807).
[39] Laurence Brockliss, John Cardwell, and Michael Moss, *Nelson's Surgeon* (Oxford, 2005), p. 150.

still on his feet, waving a sword in defiance at his enemies. Gradually, however, as the true circumstances began to emerge, the artists were forced to show a more realistic scene. But, even then, there was resistance to the idea of showing the death as it really happened, in the blood-stained, lamp-lit cockpit of the *Victory*, below the waterline, far removed from the raging battle. The President of the Royal Academy, Benjamin West, who had made his reputation more than thirty years before with one of the most famous depictions of military demise, *The Death of General Wolfe*, could not bring himself to paint Nelson's death realistically. Instead, he placed the scene on the quarterdeck of the *Victory*, which enabled him to show the admiral surrounded by all his comrades in arms, some of whom were still carrying on the fight. When challenged about the authenticity of such a treatment, he replied:

> there was no other way of representing the death of a Hero but by an Epic representation of it. . . . Nelson [should not] be represented dying in the gloomy hold of a ship, like a sick man in a Prison Hole. To move the mind there should be a spectacle presented to raise & warm the mind and all shd. be proportioned to the highest idea conceived of the Hero.[40]

West's *The Death of Nelson* has not stood the test of time and nowadays it is barely known. The most familiar depiction of the famous scene is one by Arthur Devis, now in the National Maritime Museum, which does, after all, show Nelson dying 'in the gloomy hold of a ship' and is clearly based on Beatty's account of the death. Indeed, it is so well known nowadays that, when the editor of *Radio Times* wanted a striking image for her cover to mark the passing of 'Mike Baldwin', a long-standing character in the ITV 'soap' *Coronation Street*, she chose Devis's painting as the basis for a specially posed photograph.[41] But West's heroic image was hugely popular with his contemporaries: when he displayed it in his own house, some 30,000 people viewed it within the space of a month and prints of it sold in their thousands.[42] It showed Nelson as his contemporaries wanted to see him— as the triumphant hero and not as the suffering man.

Similar tensions can also be detected in the creation of one of the main foundation stones of the Nelson Legend—the monumental biography published by the Chaplain to the Prince of Wales, the Revd James Stanier Clarke, in collaboration with John M'Arthur.[43] First announced in 1807 in

---

[40] Helmut von Erffa and Allen Staley, *The Paintings of Benjamin West* (New Haven, 1996), p. 222.

[41] *Radio Times*, 30 March 2006.

[42] Von Erffa and Staley, *The Paintings of Benjamin West*, p. 222.

[43] James Stanier Clarke and John M'Arthur, *The Life of Admiral Lord Nelson, K.B.* (London, 1809).

a prospectus highlighting that the work was 'sanctioned by Earl Nelson and his family', the book was eventually published in 1809, in two bulky volumes, with a long list of august patrons. There was little likelihood, therefore, that it would be detached or dispassionate in its treatment of Nelson's story. From the start, everyone involved was anxious that it should present The Hero in the best possible light and that it should not upset any of its numerous supporters. In M'Arthur's papers in the Rosenbach Library in Philadelphia there is a letter from Frances, Lady Nelson, dating from December 1806. She had made a number of her husband's letters available to the editors and now she was worried about a passage in one of them that she feared might offend Lord Spencer, the former First Lord of the Admiralty. She wrote, 'I am under personal obligations to Lord & Lady Spencer they were of the very few who had the independence and Virtue enough to Notice a poor deserted wife.'[44] The Nelson family also contributed some tall stories, particularly about Nelson's childhood, that have continued to be repeated in subsequent biographies and it is only recently that they have been effectively challenged and discarded by Roger Knight in his magisterial new biography.[45]

Clarke and M'Arthur furthered the creation of Nelson's heroic image with a superb set of illustrations, based on paintings commissioned from Benjamin West, leading marine artist Nicholas Pocock, and Richard Westall.[46] Most of them are now very well known, having been repeatedly reproduced in subsequent biographies, and so they have become an integral part of the Nelson Legend—indeed, it is arguable that they have influenced its development even more than the text, since the book itself is seldom read nowadays. The studies by Richard Westall, of five key moments in Nelson's career, are particularly stylized and 'heroic'. For example, in *Nelson Boarding an American Prize*, a young Lieutenant Nelson steps gracefully down into a tossing boat, at the height of a gale, without holding on—like Christ quelling the storm on Galilee.

However, Clarke and M'Arthur's most profound influence on the Legend was through their editing of Nelson's letters. Having assembled a large amount of his correspondence, they decided to construct their text by using what they called 'His Lordships own manuscripts'. Sadly, however, they were not content to let Nelson's manuscripts stand as he had written them. Instead, they edited the letters, 'improving' the grammar and style,

---

[44] Rosenbach Library, Philadelphia, Msf 1073/12.

[45] Roger Knight, *The Pursuit of Victory: The Life and Achievement of Horatio Nelson* (London, 2005).

[46] West contributed two paintings, Pocock six, and Westall five. All are now in the National Maritime Museum, Greenwich.

cutting out some passages altogether, and even taking sections from a number of different letters and combining them. It has always been known that they mishandled their material but the full extent of their depredations has only recently begun to emerge, as a result of the findings of the Nelson Letters Project, set up in 1999 by the Royal Naval Museum, to examine Nelson's correspondence and identify unpublished material.[47] For example, we now know that Nelson wrote over seventy letters to the Duke of Clarence, later William IV, whom he first met when they served together in North American waters and the West Indies in the early 1780s. Of these Clarke and M'Arthur used only half: the remaining letters were suppressed and remained unknown, and unused by biographers, until they were recently relocated. Now that they have been fully transcribed for the first time, some fascinating new material has emerged. It has also been established that even those letters that were published were heavily edited to remove confidential, or potentially embarrassing, material.[48]

In fact, the Clark and M'Arthur biography did not sell well. It cost 9 guineas and the two massive volumes weighed some 10 kilograms, which made them difficult to read without a bookstand. An abridged edition was produced in 1810 and a second edition, in three small volumes, in 1839–40, but neither was any more commercially successful than the first edition.[49] So the book's influence might well have been minimal had it not been for Robert Southey's *Life of Nelson*, published in 1813 in two small volumes. It was an instant success, has never been out of print since, and has been very influential in the development of the Nelson Legend. Southey drew extensively on Clarke and M'Arthur for his material—including their heavily edited versions of the letters and their fanciful stories of childhood prowess. Thus, because of the popularity of Southey's book, much of the spurious Clarke and M'Arthur material became enshrined in the Legend.

Immortality

Throughout all the contemporary accounts of the events following the arrival of the news of Trafalgar, one word rings clear like a bass note in a peal of bells—*immortal*. Collingwood used it in the dispatch carried by

---

[47] For a full description of the Project, and analysis of its findings, see Colin White (ed.), *Nelson: The New Letters* (Woodbridge, 2005), pp. xi–xxiv.

[48] White (ed.), *Letters*, p. xxi.

[49] Michael Nash, 'Building a Nelson library: an introduction to the "Top Twenty"', in White (ed.), *The Nelson Companion*, pp. 177–97, at p. 181.

Lapenotiere, referring to Nelson as 'a hero whose name will be immortal'.[50] It sounded repeatedly in the special verses written for the stage and printed in newspapers after the arrival of the news in England and in the sermons preached on the Day of Thanksgiving. And it echoed around the dome of St Paul's at the culmination of the elaborate state funeral, when Sir Isaac Heard ended the traditional proclamation of the titles of the deceased with the unscripted words: 'The hero who, in the moment of Victory, fell covered with immortal Glory! Let us humbly trust that he is now raised to bliss ineffable, and to a glorious immortality!'[51]

On closer examination, it becomes clear that the word was being used in two distinct senses. First, it was a classical reference. Nelson's shade is frequently pictured, in art as well as in literature, returning to watch over the fate of his country and to inspire his comrades to yet more splendid acts of heroism. Many of the poems of the time, often written by men with a classical education, take up this theme. For example, George Canning's 'Ulm and Trafalgar', quoted earlier, paints a picture of future wars when

> Thou, sacred Shade, in battle hovering near
> Shall win bright Victory from her golden sphere
> To float aloft where England's ensign lies
> With angel wings and palms from paradise![52]

Indeed, Robert Southey himself ended his *Life of Nelson* with two lines of Greek from Hesiod's *Works and Days*, which may be translated (loosely) as, 'Almighty Zeus in his great wisdom has appointed them deities; and, living still on earth, they guard and inspire poor mortal men.'[53]

Second, amidst all the tributes there is also a recognizable Christian strand. Nelson is portrayed as the saviour of his country: a man who has laid down his life for his friends. This can been seen in most of the paintings of his death: even Devis's more realistic rendition of the scene shows Nelson bathed in a heavenly aura of an intensity that no mere ship's lantern could produce and with the heavy beams of the *Victory* hinting at a cross. Most strikingly, the strand can be seen in another of Benjamin West's works, produced for the Clarke and M'Arthur biography, *The Immortality of Nelson* (Figure 2.5). In this elaborate allegorical piece the dead Nelson, naked and wrapped in a white shroud, is lifted by Neptune and Victory into the arms of a mourning Britannia.[54] The painting clearly refers to that staple of

---

[50] Nicolas, *Dispatches*, vol. 7, p. 214.
[51] *Naval Chronicle*, 15 (January–June 1806), 225.
[52] Nicolas, *Dispatches*, vol. 7, p. 357.
[53] Southey, *Life of Nelson*, vol. 2, p. 275.
[54] Von Erffa and Staley, *The Paintings of Benjamin West*, p. 225.

Figure 2.5. *The Immortality of Nelson.* Benjamin West's allegorical celebration of Nelson's apotheosis. His body is offered to a mourning Britannia by Neptune and Victory. Oil painting by Benjamin West. A line engraving by Charles Heath was published as the frontispiece to Clarke and M'Arthur's *The Life of Admiral Lord Nelson, K.B.* (London, 1809). © National Maritime Museum.

religious art, the 'Deposition from the Cross', with Nelson cast in the role of Christ.

Further evidence of this quasi-idolatrous mood of 1805–6 can be seen in the extraordinary number of Nelson's personal belongings which have survived in all the major Nelson collections. Following the arrival of the *Victory* in England, Nelson's friends, relatives, and professional colleagues were besieged with requests for mementoes, and every available item—even shirt studs and pens—became relics. Midshipman Richard Bulkeley received a letter from Captain Thomas Bertie asking for some hair and wrote on 12 December: 'I regret extremely not to be able to send as much hair as I could wish, owing to my having sent away a greater part of it; but I trust you will find sufficient for a ring.' Nelson's prize agent and close friend, Alexander Davison, sent an autograph collector, Thomas Davidson, two letter covers, 'bearing the writing of my ever to be lamented Bosom friend—the Immortal Nelson!'[55]

It was left to Britain's greatest caricaturist, James Gillray, to prick the bubble of this particular manifestation of Nelson-worship, with a wonderful satire on the excesses of contemporary mourning. In early 1806, Gillray published one of his masterpieces, the superbly drawn *Immortality—the Death of Admiral Lord Nelson—in the Moment of Victory!* (Figure 2.6). It shows Nelson dying on the quarterdeck of the *Victory* in a style very similar to the allegorical paintings by West and his colleagues. He is supported by Captain Hardy and a sailor is presenting him with a captured French flag. Behind him, Britannia is in floods of tears and, above, Fame blows on a trumpet and writes 'Immortality' on the clouds. It is only on closer examination that it becomes apparent that 'Hardy' is a caricature of George III, the 'sailor' is the Duke of Clarence—while 'Britannia' has the distinctively pretty face and ample bosom of . . . Emma Hamilton!

Conclusion

John Braham had another attempt at depicting Nelson's death. In 1811, he composed the music for *The Americans*, an opera with a libretto by Samuel Arnold. This included 'The Death of Nelson', a showy tenor solo for Braham, with dramatic musical sound effects, depicting the battle itself and building to the climactic moment when 'the fatal wound / Which spread dismay around / The hero's breast received'. This time, however, there were no cries of 'Off! Off!' On the contrary, the song was a huge success and

---

[55] Bulkeley: *Naval Chronicle* 15 (January–June 1806), 34. Davison: RNM 88/499 (14).

Figure 2.6. James Gillray, *Immortality—the Death of Admiral Lord Nelson—in the Moment of Victory! . . . Design for the Memorial Intended by the City of London*, etching (1805). © National Maritime Museum.

quickly became Braham's most celebrated performance piece for the rest of his long and distinguished career. 'The Death of Nelson' remained a staple of the tenor repertoire throughout the nineteenth century, was sung frequently during the 1905 centenary celebrations, and even enjoyed a modest revival during the bicentenary 'Trafalgar Festival' in 2005.

Only five years before the song was first performed, the audience in the King's Theatre had erupted in protest at a depiction of Nelson's death that it felt was 'too strong'—but clearly, by 1811, such a depiction was permissible, even popular. The immediate, instinctive, and subtly nuanced response to Nelson's demise had already begun to solidify into the Nelson Legend.

3.
Remembering Victory—Commemorating Defeat? The Franco-British Trafalgar Centenary in 1905

BERTRAND TAITHE

The centenary of 1905 came at the very end of a commemorative process based on first-hand human experience. In 1905 there was still a tenuous linkage to the living memory of Trafalgar. As the French wit Alphonse Allais put it, each year closer to 1900 meant that the chances of Napoleonic veterans boring you to death decreased with the increased occurrence of their own demise: 'On a beau dire, plus ça ira, et moins on rencontrera de gens ayant connu Napoléon.'[1] As a matter of fact the last survivor of the French ship *Redoutable* had died peacefully in 1892 at the age of 101.

The 1905 centenary thus meant coming to terms with the shift from memory to commemoration, from narrative iteration at first hand to the historicized participation of the public in a celebratory ceremony and, for the first time, the increased mediation and diffusion of commemoration through mechanical reproduction and the use of film. In the first part of this essay the discussion will thus revolve around the meanings of history and memory in 1905 from the viewpoint of contemporaneous commemorative policies as well as from the perspective of the subsequent historiography of memory and history in that period. The second section of the essay will concentrate on the paradoxes of remembering defeat and on the complex position of nations which had recently encountered catastrophic defeats of a magnitude dwarfing the Battle of Trafalgar. The French were still coming to terms with the consequences of the Franco-Prussian war of 1870; the Spaniards with the recent war against the United States of America and the conclusion of 400 years of imperialism. To place 1905 in that context is to enquire what exactly there is to remember in a hundred-year-old naval defeat which, for the French at least, could be balanced with other 1805 events of equal symbolic magnitude, such as the Battle of

[1] Alphonse Allais, *Pensées, textes et anecdotes* (Paris, 2000), p. 105.

Austerlitz on 2 December. From this largely historiographical perspective the essay will move to the political and diplomatic context of 1905 itself. Only one year into the renewed Franco-British alliance, the memory of the last major naval confrontation of the two world powers could have played on undesirable nationalistic tropes. Yet 1905 came early in this diplomatic setting to acquire new meanings and, through the French participation in the naval celebration, the centenary transcended jingoistic readings of the battle. Finally, the essay will explore a few aspects of the ceremonial commemoration and of its recording for posterity to illustrate how these themes were negotiated and how the British and the French came to terms with the events.

1905

In geopolitical terms 1905 appears as a crucial turning point in the Edwardian world. The Franco-British alliance of the Entente Cordiale had recently ended a latent rivalry which could have found in the colonial setting a reason for war as it had nearly done some seven years earlier after the Fashoda incident, when the French and British clashed in their rapid appropriation of Africa. In 1898, a mission led by Commandant Marchand had met Kitchener's force in a potentially explosive confrontation.[2] The settlement had paved the way for the pragmatic Entente Cordiale over European and colonial interests. The 1905 Russian defeat and subsequent revolution had revealed further the weakness of the key Continental ally of the French republic, while the major battle of Tsushima recalled Trafalgar and underlined the importance of modern naval warfare. In naval history, 1905 is a turning point in the re-armament race led by the British navy. In France, 1905 was also the year of the dismantling of the Napoleonic religious consensus. The long-expected separation of churches and state took a dramatic turn and alienated from the republic the Catholics who had attempted a brief *ralliement* since the mid-1890s. Divided within, the Third Republic was seeking a firm alliance against its German rivals: Trafalgar commemorations were to enable a joint celebration of ninety years of peace and occasional alliance with Britain. Yet the French participation in the celebrations of 1905 went against the grain of the French historiography and commemoration of 1805 even while it fitted with a well-established pattern of memorialization of past conflicts.

[2] Darrell Bates, *The Fashoda Incident of 1898: Encounter on the Nile* (Oxford, 1984).

History and Memory: Trafalgar and Austerlitz

The relationship between history and memory was not a novelty in any sense and the issue had been raised powerfully by the generation immediately following the Napoleonic era. Yet over the previous thirty years a considerable shift had already taken place in the remembrance of war victims across Europe. Monuments to the dead had been built in the period 1870–90 in France; more recently the British had also engaged in localized monumental representations of grief for the numerous casualties of the Boer War. This monumental commemorative process—also found in Germany after the 1870 war with France—belonged to a more general process of nation-making acts of remembrance sketched out by George Mosse; it also relates to the historiography of commemorative acts of the war dead which started in earnest with the work of Jay Winter.[3] These monumental embodiments of the national duty of grieving and celebrating had their precedents in the more abstract hero-worship of Nelson, Napoleon, and Wellington. Even the collective narration of war deeds found in the Arc de Triomphe at the Louvre and on the Champs Élysées, the Colonne Vendôme and in Nelson's Column, or the funerals given to all three war leaders, remained allegorical. These precedents presented a very concentrated vision of grieving, focusing primarily on the leader and on the revival of ancient modes of celebrations, often making direct parallels with antiquity by evoking models such as Trajan's Column or referring directly to classical heroes.[4] In contrast, the commemorative acts of the late nineteenth century did not venture beyond passing neo-classical architectural references. Instead they were meant to be nominally inclusive, with long lists of the war dead presented to the public in print or inscribed on monuments. The first monuments to the dead in France after 1871 were thus printed lists of names,[5] followed by the creation of national monuments and regional lists.[6] The debates over memory in France were particularly focused on a secular–religious divide. The Catholic Church presented its

---

[3] Exemplary of the extremely rich and developed historiography are George L. Mosse, *Fallen Soldiers: Reshaping the Memory of the World Wars* (Oxford, 1990); Jay Winter, *Sites of Memory, Sites of Mourning: The Great War in European Cultural History* (Cambridge, 1995); Bertrand Taithe, *Defeated Flesh: Welfare, Warfare, and the Making of Modern France* (Manchester, 1999).

[4] See, for a comparative analysis, Maurice Griffe, *La Campagne de 1805 (Austerlitz) racontée par la colonne Vendôme* (Paris, 1998). On Trajan's Column: www.stoa.org/trajan/.

[5] Paul d'Albigny, *Le Livre d'or du département de l'Ardèche, contenant la liste des enfants de ce département morts en 1870–1871* (n.p., 1879).

[6] Émile Bader, *Mars-la-Tour et son monument national* (Mars-la-Tour, 1893); Clément de Lacroix, *Les Morts pour la patrie: tombes militaires et monuments élevés à la mémoire des soldats tués pendant la guerre. Chronologie historique des événements de 1870–1871* (n.p., 1891).

own alternative readings of French history since the revolution and in buildings such as the Sacré-Coeur of Montmartre offered commemorative ex-votos which remembered the dead and usually reiterated tropes of sacrifice for the glory of God rather than the nation.[7] Nevertheless, even within this alternative model of representation of the dead, the individual soldier became increasingly the focus of grieving and commemoration.

What Nora entitled 'the psychological turn of the nineteenth century' made room for the grief of individual families.[8] Meanwhile the historical machinery of the nineteenth century had developed to its full potential the narrative techniques that made sense of the Napoleonic conflicts as well as of the most recent wars. Historians, imitating Balzacian novelists, had developed the godly stature that enabled them to narrate the intentions as well as the design of war heroes, frequently attributing design to lucky occurrences and making sense of the battles in often exaggeratedly orderly narratives.[9] Though a few such as Michelet had attempted to grant the people centre stage in their frescoes,[10] most had followed in the footsteps of Adolphe Thiers and concentrated on the leaders.[11] The recent Rankean shift in the methodological paradigm of history writing gave new legitimacy to the study of plans and high-level politics.

From the French perspective the historiography of the military history of the Revolution and Empire remained dominated by the shadow of Adolphe Thiers. Thiers had been a formidable player in French politics from his days during the Orléans Regime. His brand of liberal nationalism rested largely on his desire to reutilize the Bonapartist story to establish a nationalist legend and find popular support for the regime while working towards the ending of the Vienna System, which had so completely isolated France on the international scene. The subsequent revolutions of 1830 and the aftershock of 1832 had reinforced the image of France as a land of troublemakers.[12] Thus the Orléans Regime in 1840 brought back to Paris the corpse of Napoleon and staged a state funeral of unprece-

[7] R. A. Jones, 'Monuments as ex-voto, monuments as historiography: the basilica of Sacré Coeur', *French Historical Studies*, 18/2 (1993), 482–502.

[8] Pierre Nora, *Lieux de mémoires*, 2 vols, 2nd edn (Paris, [1993] 1997).

[9] Only Tolstoy avoided that trick but this had been also anticipated in Stendhal, *La Chartreuse de Parme*; see Bruno Latour, *The Pasteurisation of France* (Cambridge, Mass., 1993).

[10] Jules Michelet, *Histoire de la révolution française*, 2nd edn (Paris, 1868–9); in the same vein: Jean Jaurès, *Histoire socialiste de la révolution française*, 3 vols (Paris, 1895–1905).

[11] Adolphe Thiers, *Histoire du consulat et de l'Empire*, 10 vols (Paris, 1845–51).

[12] F. M. Atkinson (ed.), *Memoirs of M. Thiers, 1870–1873* (London, 1915); Adolphe Thiers, *Occupation et liberation du territoire, 1871–1873: Correspondances*, 2 vols (Paris, 1903); John Patrick T. Bury and Robert P. Tombs, *Thiers 1797–1877: A Political Life* (London, 1986); Anon. (ed.), *Monsieur Thiers: d'une république à l'autre* (Marseilles, 1998).

dented importance while also completing the monumental commemoration of Napoleonic victories. The revolution of 1848 further developed the myth when Napoleon's nephew, Louis Napoleon, came to embody Bonaparte's legend. Thiers was once again important in supporting this figure before the two drifted apart. Thiers put the final touch to the historical account of the First Empire which would remain central in its subtle mixture of admiration and condemnation for a great man whose will had been corrupted by power. In the same way that Victor Hugo had used the comparison between Napoleon I and Napoleon III to condemn 'Napoléon le petit', Thiers established a narrative which saw Napoleon drift from being the incarnation of the national genius, much in the same manner as Carlyle had perceived him, to being a despot.[13] In that narrative, 1805 served as the *annus mirabilis* of the regime, as the year of triumph for both the French military genius and its leader. Ulm and Austerlitz more than compensated for the naval disaster of Trafalgar, and their strategic importance seemed much greater to Thiers than a defeat which could only with hindsight be seen to have real significance.[14] From that perspective Thiers associated the remembrance of a sequence of battles—Trafalgar, Ulm, and Austerlitz. This association has proved durable both in their centenary and bicentenary, yet, on both occasions the state commemorated Trafalgar less hesitantly than the Napoleonic victories, particularly Austerlitz.[15]

On Trafalgar itself, Thiers had favoured two sets of explanations for the defeat: a psychological one and a material one. The former was concentrated on Napoleon's lack of trust in Villeneuve's ability. The latter focused on the under-investment in the fleet, which had meant that while the ships were sound the sailors were not; this explained the subsequent cowardice if not betrayal of most of the Spanish fleet and of some of the French fleet.[16] Ultimately, Thiers described the battle as a Pyrrhic victory for the British, stressing the disastrous storm, during which the *Bucentaure* and the *Algesiras* managed to escape, and the subsequent rescue of the *Santa Anna* and *Neptuno*. Ultimately 'unhappy courage is not less admirable than the victorious one: it is more moving. As a matter of fact the good fortunes of

---

[13] Thomas Carlyle, *On Heroes, Hero Worship, and the Heroic in History* (London, [1840] 1873), pp. 218–21.

[14] In fact this analysis is retained even in recent works such as Edward Ingram, 'Illusions of victory: the Nile, Copenhagen, and Trafalgar revisited', *Military Affairs*, 48/2 (1984), 140–3.

[15] George A. Furse, *A Hundred Years Ago. Battles by Land and By Sea: Ulm, Trafalgar, Austerlitz* (London, 1905).

[16] This point was virulently criticized south of the Pyrenees: Carlos Creus, *Carta dirigida al Sr. D. Augusto Thiers por D. Carlos Creus, refutando las infundadas é injustas acusaciones que dirige á marinos españoles que combatieron en Trafalgar* (Madrid, 1851). See Ronald J. Quirk, *Literature as Introspection: Spain Confronts Trafalgar* (London, 1998).

France were such [in 1805] that one could admit some of fate's harsher treatments.'[17]

The first point, on under-investment, has to be contextualized in the mid-nineteenth century politics in which these accounts were inserted.[18] Thiers had been a major force in the remilitarization of France in the 1830s and 1840s and it was to a large extent the Orleanist army which fought the war in the Crimea. The emphasis on the navy had some urgency in the 1840s as Britain was then also renewing its sea defences against a possible French invasion. From a French viewpoint, investment in the navy only made sense at the time of an acute rivalry with Britain, and on the basis of an established superiority on land. The shifts in the power balance of continental Europe from 1864 onwards made that investment relatively less meaningful, and French naval strategic thinking was dominated by the Nouvelle école, which attempted to cash in on technological developments to counter the superiority of the British navy by developing a rapid, aggressive, and skirmishing fleet. The Nouvelle école reflected the French lack of durable commitment to the navy at a moment of political uncertainty. In 1870, in spite of its incontestable superiority the French navy had had little impact against the German coalition. Its forces served primarily on land and found glory in the defence of Sedan, with examples of heroic if futile resistance such as the 'house of the last cartridges' in Balan and Bazeilles, and in the defence of Paris with its naval guns.[19] The war never took place on sea. Subsequent developments in French naval thinking had been muddled by conflicting colonial and European priorities which accorded more or less importance to the offensive anti-British naval strategy of the Nouvelle école. Ironically, 1905 and the Russo-Japanese war restated the importance of the decisive naval battle precisely at the time when the Entente Cordiale made the perspective of an actual conflict with Britain unlikely.[20]

With the new alliance in place and with a junior role implicitly devolved to the French navy, the lessons of 1805 that mattered most in the teaching of the École militaire and École de guerre remained those of Ulm and Austerlitz. For the École supérieure de la marine created in 1896, the dogmatic role of the decisive battle was framed in a historical analysis that included the battles of the Nile and Trafalgar. Politically, participation

[17] Thiers, *Histoire*, vol. 4, pp. 182–3.
[18] These views still dominate the French historiography: see for instance Michèle Battesti, *Trafalgar: les aléas de la stratégie navale de Napoléon* (Paris, 2004).
[19] Bazeilles took place on 31 August and became the commemorative day of French marines. Georges Bastard, *La Défense de Bazeilles* (Ollendorff, 1884); Abbot Fouquet, *Bazeilles pendant la guerre* (Balan-Sedan, 1895); George Hooper, *The Campaign of Sedan: The Downfall of the Second Empire, August–September 1870*, 2nd edn (London, 1897), pp. 316–17.
[20] Richard Hill, *La Guerre maritime—la marine à vapeur, 1855–1905* (Paris, 2003), pp. 61, 91.

in a celebration of Trafalgar became less problematic than a celebration of the victory of a Bonaparte. In some respects the commemorative acts of defeat had acquired an emotional intensity in post-1870 France that the more triumphant ceremonies of 2 December lacked. The fact that the École militaire of Saint Cyr had taken 2 December as its main day of celebrations since the mid-Second Empire only reinforced the impression that the French army might not be entirely republican. The relevance of Bonapartism in France in 1905 was still acute, as was a general distrust of high-ranking officers. In November 1904, the 'affaire des fiches', revealed by the Parisian nationalistic daily, *Le Figaro*, showed that the government of Combes was monitoring its officers' religious beliefs with the help of the anti-clerical obedience of the Freemasonry of the Grand Orient of France.[21] By early 1905 the Combes government fell in the aftermath of the controversy. This context is revealing, especially when one knows that the nickname of the French navy, to this day, is 'la Royale'—a reference to its origins and assumed political leanings.

Commemorating Defeat

What made the 1905 commemoration of Trafalgar unique was the fact that the French participated willingly in the remembering of their greatest naval defeat. Acts of commemorating defeat are deeply embedded in a specific political context in which different narrative modes compete to present meaningful sequences of heroic deeds, which, in their individual glory, balance the disastrous effects of the whole. The Franco-Prussian War, endlessly serialized in the newspapers around 1900, was thus made more meaningful by the multitude of anecdotes that reflected the courage and honour of some men in some situations. In many instances these sacrificial themes, arguably central to French politics by that stage, were 'privatized' by an organization or a site to promote *esprit de corps* or a sense of belonging.[22]

In the French army a number of defeats were thus commemorated for the heroism of the men sent to certain death or to willing sacrifice by their commanders. The Foreign Legion celebrated (and still celebrates) the Mexican defeat of Camerone Hacienda in Mexico, on 29 April 1863, when

---

[21] François Vindé, *L'Affaire des fiches, 1900–1904: chroniques d'un scandale* (Paris, 1989).

[22] The sacrificial themes have been explored controversially in Richard D. E. Burton, *Blood in the City: Violence and Revelation in Paris, 1789–1945* (Ithaca, NY, 2001), Ivan Strenski, *Contesting Sacrifice: Religion, Nationalism, and Social Thought in France* (Chicago, 2002), and most recently Jesse Goldhammer, *The Headless Republic: Sacrificial Violence in Modern French Thought* (Ithaca, NY, 2005).

a group of sixty men resisted around 2,000 Mexican soldiers for eleven hours. The name of the battle was put on the flag of the Foreign Legion, the name of the commanding officers added to the lists of the Invalides monument in Paris, and a monument to their memory erected *in situ* in 1892. From 1864 onwards Camerone Day became the day of celebration of the Foreign Legion. More recently, and on the same narrative lines, the defence of Bazeilles and Balan near Sedan by French marines (*troupes de marines*) remained a vivid symbol of military valour glorified in paintings and annual celebration.[23] Cities like Belfort commemorated their resistance in monumental terms, and villages like Mars-La-Tour made their more humble monument to the dead sites of nationalistic pilgrimages between 1871 and 1914.

These commemorations of defeats, each of them relatively insignificant by itself, enabled a considerable revival in patriotism and militarism in France which the Dreyfus Affair had recently undermined.[24] The structural issues which caused defeat had, the French public was assured, been dealt with primarily by reforms of the training of commanding officers in imitation of German methods.[25] Within that context the significance of Waterloo could be minimized by the sheer imbalance of the forces in the war and commemorated as a glorious day by recalling the suicidal conduct of the old guard. The Battle of Trafalgar was more complex from a French perspective. Of course there had been a number of gallant acts from a number of sailors—notably aboard the *Redoutable*—but Villeneuve's command had been lacklustre and much of the fleet had barely seen action. The release of Lucas's memoirs in 1886 had enabled a new emphasis on the *Redoutable*'s exploits against vastly superior enemies. The reading of the memoir to the old Provencal survivor, *le père* Cortigni, was recorded in 1890 and subsequently reprinted until 1914. The sentimental anecdote clearly stated in the survivor's own words:

> When I got my senses again, I found myself amongst the dead and the dying and all sorts of rubbish and I learned that, after winning our battle against the *Victory* we had succumbed to a carnage inflicted by two other enemy ships . . . [T]ell me please my good man what happened while I fainted.[26]

---

[23] Taithe, *Defeated Flesh*, ch. 1.

[24] Paul B. Miller, *From Revolutionaries to Citizens: Antimilitarism in France, 1870–1914* (Durham and London, 2002).

[25] Allan Mitchell, *Victors and Vanquished: The German Influence on Army and Church in France after 1870* (Chapel Hill, NC, 1984).

[26] Commandant Lucas, *La Bataille de Trafalgar racontée par le commandant Lucas avec les impressions du dernier survivant de ce combat, le Père Cortigni* (Toulon, [1891] 1914), reprinted in Anon., *Trafalgar et la marine du premier Empire* (Paris, 2001), p. 51.

As the survivor pointed out, there was heroism and even partial victory in defeat and the killing of Nelson could serve as compensation for the ultimate defeat. Trafalgar is a singularly complex battle to commemorate, as both sides can stress losses and glory. Nelson was central to any commemorative event as a victim of war, killed by the hand of the French, who were themselves victims of his 'transcendental genius'. Meanwhile his stature as a sea officer grew to become heroic. Nelson had been shot in action and his sacrifice, which included his famous prayer and signal, enabled an allegorical reading of the battle. The combination of the text of the prayer and the legend of the parade uniform[27] made Nelson a new Publius Decius Mus, the Roman generals who had sacrificed themselves in an act of *devotio* to ensure the victory of their cause.[28] This particular allegorical dimension alone enabled the celebration of Trafalgar as a great heroic deed, undoubtedly grounded in historical circumstances but transcending the geopolitical context of the early nineteenth century. The historiography of the Battle of Trafalgar had thus to contend with the mytheme of the sacrificial general,[29] as well as the more complex historiography of the Napoleonic wars. Trafalgar prefigured Waterloo from a British point of view, but also St Helena from a French one. The sacrificial and eschatological dimensions of Nelson's death related to what Lucien Febvre called the honour and fatherland (*patrie*) nexus, which represented a dialectical relationship between an individual and a collective, between ideal models and the ethical foundations of self-governance.[30] The honour of a group, the navy for instance, could thus transcend patriotic boundaries while relating to the national form, the British navy. In nationalist discourse, be it in Catholic models of sacrifice or in the British models of heroism, heroic deaths symbolized the primacy of duty over rights, the bulwark of social binds and group solidarity against the dissolving influence of divisive class politics.

Yet to commemorate the man Nelson in 1905 was not without some complex implications. Undoubtedly the figure of Nelson could feature in the character-building literature for children, but some aspects of his

---

[27] Colin White, 'Nelson apotheosised: the creation of the Nelson Legend', in David Cannadine (ed.), *Admiral Lord Nelson: Context and Legacy* (London, 2005), pp. 93–114, at p. 94.
[28] The three generals, all known as Publius Decius Mus, sacrificed themselves in the battles of Vesuvius, Sentinum, and Asculum respectively. Their story was well known from Livy (8.6, 9–10) and had been represented in a series of paintings by Rubens (copies of which are still available from commercial artists, see www.oceansbridge.com/oil-paintings/product. php?xProd=2080&xSec=11 (accessed 6 January 2006)) and by Fragonard in 1774 and was a commonplace in neo-classical allegories of heroism.
[29] Joseph Hammond, *Every Man, His Duty: The Lessons of Trafalgar and its Hero. A Sermon for the Nelson Centenary* (London, 1905); id., *Nelson and Trafalgar: The Man and the Deed* (London, 1905).
[30] Lucien Febvre, *Honneur et patrie* (Paris, 1996).

character, including his womanizing and vainglory, were not necessarily good pedagogic stock. Yet, as numerous historians have noted, certain of Nelson's characteristics, especially his insistence on action, fitted best with Edwardian manly types which were not purely British. The hero Nelson was transmogrified through his death and a teleology which enabled a simplified figure to emerge whose message had more universality than jingoistic undertones. In 1905, however, the two messages echoed forcefully and the jingoistic figure remained very potent. For French commentators, the figure of Nelson was darkened by his behaviour in Naples, though blame was commonly shifted to Lady Hamilton. The major biographical sources mediated in French encyclopaedic dictionaries were Robert Southey's *Life of Nelson* (2nd edition, 1813) and Nelson's correspondence edited by Thomas Pettigrew (1849), as well as the Harris–Nicolas edition of Nelson's dispatches and letters (1844–6).[31] While Southey remained in print and served well the Nelsonian legend in Britain, there was much in its language that could wake the old rivalry even after editing.[32] Variously described as perfidious, cruel, and lacking honour and humanity, the French appeared singularly opposed to the gentlemanly qualities of Nelson and his men in Southey's prose.[33]

From a French perspective, representations of the French side were equally complex. Napoleon presented the force of a genius, the dangers of 'Caesarism', and the cult of personality that the Third Republic jealously guarded itself from by denying any of its dominant figureheads genuine lasting power.[34] From the point of view of the battle rather than the leader, it was the plan, the decisive and unpredictable action, which retained a certain currency. In French 'le coup de Trafalgar' acquired the meaning of a surprise decisive act, on a par with the 'coup de Jarnac', which referred to the underhand duelling technique of Sire Jarnac at the court of Henri II. The phrase has remained in continuous use since at least the mid-nineteenth century and, in the jargon of the Tour de France, created in 1902, a 'coup de Trafalgar' denotes a surprise attack undertaken strategically at an unpredictable moment and in an unprepossessing section of the race. Embedded thus in the fabric of French culture, it is perhaps less surprising to find that the centenary involved considerable French participation.

---

[31] See for instance the conservative *Dictionnaire encyclopédique de Jules Trousset* (Paris, 1900).

[32] Robert Southey, *The Battle of Trafalgar*, ed. A. C. Curtis (London, 1905).

[33] Robert Southey, *The Life of Nelson* (London, c.1906), p. 304. I am using the presentation copy awarded to a J. E. Thorpe as a prize by the Lancashire public school of Rossall in July 1907.

[34] The prime example at that time had been Gambetta, whose stay in power lasted only a few months in spite of his dominant political stature. Clemenceau in 1905 was equally feared for the same reason.

Having stated all this, the celebration of 1905 came at a crucial moment in both the history of Europe and the history of commemorative acts. Strictly speaking, by 1905 living memory was getting out of reach while private memory of Trafalgar—mostly limited to the relatively narrow confines of naval enthusiasts, the navy itself, and the surroundings of the *Victory*—became of national and international importance.[35]

Alfred J. West (1857–1937), recently rescued from relative obscurity by his great grandson David Clover, was a privileged witness of this phenomenon. West, a pioneer of sea photography and film, had developed contacts with the royal family and with the navy, on whose behalf he had composed a number of propaganda shows, which he exhibited simultaneously at various provincial and metropolitan sites, including at the London Polytechnic and in the Crystal Palace. The most successful of these shows, entitled *Our Navy*, had a particularly long run of fourteen years and combined very effectively sound effects, commentaries, acting, and stirring music.[36] Filmed in 1898, only three years after the first films of the Lumière brothers, the show had the support of the Admiralty and the Navy League.[37] West's association with both institutions proved fruitful and financially rewarding, as he developed new and more elaborate recruitment films and subsequent propaganda shows up to the eve of the Great War, as well as the occasional private film for the royal family, such as that devoted to the Duke of York's cruise aboard the *Ophir*.[38] In 1905, West found himself at the heart of the Trafalgar commemorations—not least in making propaganda films entitled *Our Navy of the Past*, one of which survives to this day.[39] This surviving short film illustrates a precise moment when mnemotechnics developed new forms and when the veteran of ninety-two—born in 1813, seven years after the battle itself, but old enough to have served with Admiral Parker, who had been at Trafalgar—could serve as a bridge between the youth of his day and the youth he had been when meeting actual veterans.[40] The film shows an elderly man walking slowly and painfully to the deck of the *Victory*, wiping his forehead, helped by three sailors of approximately the

[35] See John M. MacKenzie, 'Nelson goes global: the Nelson myth in Britain and beyond', in Cannadine (ed.), *Admiral Lord Nelson*, pp. 144–65, at p. 156. In the same volume, Colin White, 'Nelson apotheosised', points out that the Queen, passing through Portsmouth, had to be told that it was Trafalgar Day on seeing the *Victory* adorned with commemorative mourning decorations (p. 109).

[36] Alfred J. West, *Sea Salts and Celluloid* (Portsmouth, 1936), unpublished excerpt on http://mcs.open.ac.uk/dac3/ournavy/seasalts.pdf. Courtesy of David Clover.

[37] West, *Sea Salts*, p. 17.

[38] Ibid., p. 30.

[39] See on the Internet the relevant film clip with kind authorization of www.ournavy.org.uk and the Wessex Sound and Video Archives.

[40] West, *Sea Salts*, p. 33.

same age as the two young boys featured on the monument to Nelson in St Paul's Cathedral.[41] The old man, figuring as an allegory of the old navy, is shown contemplating the ship itself and turning to Nelson's famous message, 'England expects every man will do his duty.' Another film, of a Trafalgar gun seen in action, as well as lantern slides, were included in the centenary programme of *Our Navy*. The film captured an intergenerational encounter which stressed both the distance between 1805 and 1905 and their proximity. Undeniably moving, it was a great success both in London and throughout the provinces. It represented the combination of old and new mnemotechnics while relying on the pathos of intergenerational dialogue. The film was tapping into a mode of historical narration that was focused on the death of the hero and on memory rather than a jingoistic recounting of the full scale of the victory. In spite of Clowes's fictional account, there was very little expectation that the battle should ever be refought against the French.[42] The Admiralty deemed the film suitable for presentation to 1,500 French sailors and officers of the French squadron present in Portsmouth for Trafalgar Day. The addition of the two national flags, the national anthems, and a few slides in French provoked a suitably cordial response.[43] The Gunnery school of HMS *Excellent* had earlier welcomed the French squadron with a choreography forming the message 'Vive la France' on the banks of Whale Island.

The film was also shown at the Crystal Palace, the People's Palace, and the Royal Albert Hall in aid of the British and Foreign Sailors' Society. Interestingly, the ceremony at the Albert Hall involved the sending of a wreath and a bust of Nelson to Admiral Togo of Japan, the victor of Tsushima, who was commonly compared to Nelson.[44] By associating Togo and the recent conflict with Nelson, the organizers undoubtedly wished to enshrine the international importance of the British hero. Again, that ceremony commemorated Nelson and his death rather than the French defeat:

> At 3 o'clock the vast audience stood up and sang the hymn 'All people that on earth do dwell' after which the Revd. Canon Barker chaplain to the king offered an appropriate prayer. Mrs Tree then recited Rudyard Kipling's much

---

[41] See Holger Hoock, 'Nelson entombed: the military and Naval pantheon in St Paul's Cathedral', in Cannadine (ed.), *Admiral Lord Nelson*, pp. 115–43, at pp. 135–7.

[42] Sir William Laird Clowes and Sir Alan Hughes Burgoyne, *Trafalgar Refought* (London, 1905).

[43] West, *Sea Salts*, p. 33.

[44] Admiral Sir Nathaniel Bowden-Smith KCB made the same parallel, as well as the usual comments on the alliance with France, in his discussion of Trafalgar during a debate at the Institution of Naval Architects (19 July 1905). For the Nelson–Togo comparison see also John MacKenzie in Chapter 4 below.

treasured recessional.[45] On the platform was the oak timber from the 'Victory' and presented by the Lords Commissioners of the Admiralty to the British and Foreign Sailors' society. On it were the words in faded gilt: 'Here Nelson Died'.

By the side was a flagpole, and at the exact moment, when, one hundred years before, Nelson had breathed out his heroic soul in the 'Victory', an English sailor boy hoisted the Union Jack to half mast; after a brief silence Mr Ben Davies sang the 'Death of Nelson', and the flag was mast-headed.[46]

The entire ceremony was presided over by Thomas Brassey (editor of the *Naval Annual* and later warden of the Cinque Ports and created an earl) and the Lord Mayor of London. It concluded with 'God Save the King' and 'La Marseillaise'. The commemoration of Trafalgar was thus carefully combining the post-Boer War mood of commemoration with a desire to find in the death of Nelson some heroic model of masculine behaviour. Central to this were the exhibition of relics and the fetishism attached to the objects related to Trafalgar which had begun with Emma Hamilton herself and now began to feature in curated exhibitions.[47] At a fundamental level the Battle of Trafalgar had to be commemorated in association with fragments of the *Victory* itself. Unlike land battles, there was not a single site that could be identified; the battle site remained fluid and movable. Ultimately, *Victory* had become the site of Trafalgar and its timber could be displaced and bring, even to the heart of London, an authentic site of mourning. Furthermore, the production of relics from the wood or copper of *Victory*'s fabric enabled new forms of appropriation of the battle as well as fundraising for the British and Foreign Sailors' Society (Figure 3.1).

The pathos of the battle lent itself to a number of musical interpretations and dramatizations.[48] Public use of reflective poetry sometimes contrasted with more stirring private commemorative efforts, such as Hugh Blair's composition for chorus and orchestra, *Trafalgar*, which used the poem of Francis T. Palgrave (1824–97) and was described by the *Musical Times* as full of virility: '[It] abounds in contrasts—from the strenuous unaccompanied phrase "England expects every man will do his duty" to the tender

---

[45] 'God of our fathers, known of old / Lord of our far-flung battle-line / Beneath whose awful Hand we hold / Dominion over palm and pine—/ Lord God of Hosts, be with us yet, / Lest we forget—lest we forget! / The tumult and the shouting dies.' R. Kipling (1897).

[46] West, *Sea Salts*, p. 34. 'The Death of Nelson', words by Samuel James Arnold and music by John Braham, was first performed in 1811.

[47] Lieutenant-Colonel A. Leetham, *Catalogue of the Exhibition of Nelson Relics in Commemoration of the Centenary of the Battle of Trafalgar* (London, 1905). Other ephemerals appear in various catalogues: *A Souvenir of Trafalgar: 1805–1905* [With illustrations.] (London, 1905); C. W., *Souvenir of Nelson: Centenary of Trafalgar, 1805–1905* (London, 1905).

[48] Cyril Meir Scott and T. Hardy, *Trafalgar*, Opus 38, No. 2 (London, 1904).

Figure 3.1. Medal commemorating the Trafalgar Centenary, 1905 (artist unknown). Obverse and reverse. Copper, 16 mm. The inscription on the reverse claims that the medal contains 'VICTORY COPPER'. © National Maritime Museum.

music of "features that ne'er can be gazed on again till the death pang is o'er" '—but it could be played in just fifteen minutes.[49] Self-promoting authors and composers attempted to use the Nelson anniversary for commercial purposes.[50] In France and Spain the literary outpouring was lesser but included the same range of works; *L'Illustration* devoted an entire issue to the commemoration.[51]

The 1905 event was thus a dual process of nationalization of the commemoration of the Battle of Trafalgar, largely through the efforts of the Navy League and through the establishment of the event as a transnational milestone in the history of naval warfare, but also by focusing on Nelson as the model Christian naval officer. The Navy League's commemorative service at Trafalgar Square served its ambition to render all things nautical more prominent in national consciousness[52] while building on post-Boer War heroic emulation and character building.[53] The maimed body of Nelson and his sacrificial role ensured that this message could be heard beyond Britain: Nelson—while undoubtedly the archetypal *British* hero—could also be appropriated from as far away as Japan. In this context French participation in 1905 was perhaps less surprising or contradictory than it might have seemed.

Epilogue

The bicentenary in 2005 presented similar challenges to the French state as the centenary in 1905 had done. It contributed more forcefully to the Trafalgar ceremonies of June 2005 than it did to any Austerlitz ceremony in December that year. In its public relations, the French navy was particularly keen to stress its close collaboration with the Royal Navy. The ceremony on board HMS *Vanguard* between the First Sea Lord Sir Alan West and CEMMF (chef d'état-major de la Marine Française) Jean-Louis Battet

---

[49] *The Musical Times*, 46 (1 August 1905), 540.

[50] The list is too long to give in full, but see E. Derry, *Patriotic Poems in Commemoration of the Centenary of the Battle of Trafalgar* (London, 1905); Sir Henry John Newbolt, *The Year of Trafalgar: Being an Account of the Battle and of the Events which led up to it, with a Collection of the Poems and Ballads Written Thereupon between 1805 and 1905* (London, 1905); Frederick W. Pfander Swinborne, *Trafalgar Day, 1905, and Nelson Memorial Sonnets*, 2nd edn (Coggeshall, Essex, 1905).

[51] Albert Malo, *Le Centenaire de Trafalgar, 1805–1905* (Senlis, 1905).

[52] *Daily Mail*, 23 October 1905. See also Andrew S. Thompson, *Imperial Britain: The Empire in British Politics c.1880–1932* (London, 2000), p. 46. I am grateful to Ian Field for this reference. Incidentally, Kipling's recessional was employed in Trafalgar Square too.

[53] Stefan Collini, *Public Moralists: Political Thought and Intellectual Life in Britain, 1850–1930* (Oxford, 1991).

emphasized collaboration past and future, including the joint construction of aircraft carriers.[54] The *Charles de Gaulle* was the largest ship among the multinational flotilla commemorating Trafalgar at Portsmouth. Meanwhile on 2 December in Brno, an American re-enactor played Napoleon for a French army largely composed of British, German, and other European re-enactors, much to the chagrin of the smaller numbers of their French counterparts, whom the French state had not sponsored. *L'Alsace–Le Pays* titled it 'Coup de Trafalgar pour les Grognards!',[55] and denounced French unwillingness to partake officially in international commemorations of the Battle of Austerlitz on 2 December 2005.

In Paris, the 2 December ceremony near the Place Vendôme was intimate and devoid of major political representation. Of course, the political threat of Bonapartism has long ceased to be the motivation for this neglect of Austerlitz, but recent community politics and in particular the vigorous campaigning of French West Indians ensured that the tainted image of Napoleon as the ruler who had re-established slavery remained unredeemable in the public eye even at the time of the commemoration of his greatest triumph.[56]

---

[54] See the website of the French Navy: www.corlobe.tk/article884.html (accessed 3 January 2006).

[55] *L'Alsace–Le Pays*, 8 December 2005.

[56] Claude Ribbe's extremely controversial book, *Le Crime de Napoléon* (Paris, 2005), which brought together many debates on Napoleon's role in the re-establishment of slavery in the West Indies, is a recent example of the political instrumentalization of history in French identity politics. For the ambiguous French attitudes towards Napoleonic commemoration see also Peter Hicks, Chapter 7 below.

4.

Nelson the Hero and Horatio the Lover: Projections of the Myth in Canada, the Cinema, and Culture

JOHN M. MACKENZIE

The significance of the myth of Nelson as a great, perhaps the greatest, hero of the British pantheon lies in its combination of national, imperial, and international dimensions as well as in its capacity to appeal powerfully across class lines. This paper will examine these multiple resonances in respect of both Britain and Canada, the latter being used as a key example of the power of the Nelson legend within the 'British World'. It will also shift the focus to the treatment of Nelson in film in the twentieth century. These two are connected inasmuch as film became a great international medium: films made on one continent were shown in others. The iconography and ideas previously conveyed in conventional settings like outdoor ceremonies, public meetings, recreations of events, commemorative services, the unveiling of monuments and statues, and the printed ephemera and newspaper reports that went along with these, could now be powerfully represented in the medium of celluloid. Images could be converted into full-blown narratives, at one and the same time heightening the romantic power of the legend and also bringing it closer to everyday experience. Moreover, through film, the Nelson story was taken over in other European countries, notably in Germany. Film was also a strikingly cross-class medium: once its popularity was swiftly established in the years before the First World War, it was an entertainment form which drew in audiences from upper to lower classes. It was also soon recognized by politicians as having great propaganda power. Messages of national import, particularly in time of war, could be conveyed with great authority through film, and its popularity ensured that such ideas would reach the widest possible constituency.

In the course of the nineteenth century, Nelson became a major imperial hero. In many ways he established a pattern of legendary endeavour, elevated to the status of myth, which was later to be followed by David Livingstone, Henry Havelock, and Charles Gordon, with many lesser figures such as Frederick Selous, H. H. Kitchener, Baden-Powell, and T. E. Lawrence attempting (sometimes self-consciously) to enter the heroic Valhalla.[1] My study of these figures began some twenty years ago when I realized that there was a significant gap in the treatment of such historical personalities.[2] They had excited the attention of modern biographers who were building upon the multiple hagiographies that had been published after their deaths. But much less attention had been paid to the fact that these 'heroes' had to be represented in two realms: first, the life itself, in which more recent writers had tried to seek out their version of the truth, including details of private and sexual lives that had previously been obscured. But the second, and highly important, realm had scarcely been entered. This was the afterlife and half-life of the myth. Each of these figures had been inflated to legendary proportions, and it was soon apparent that these myths were highly malleable for contemporary purposes, that they developed, in other words, lives of their own. They were also significantly instrumental. They became the equivalent of the appeal to the ancestors in which the legendary name was repeatedly invoked for a whole variety of causes, for youth training, as a rod to castigate governments, as a means of promoting one policy rather than another. Such myths were not of course based upon untruths: they were elaborate embroideries upon and developments of what were perceived to be major truths. And of course they could only be built upon genuinely emblematic figures; for myths can only be grounded in great deeds that seem to be truly national, or even international, in their import.

We should remember that such myths are generated in almost all societies across the globe. There have been significant studies of this phenom-

---

[1] One of Kitchener's names was Horatio, which he 'inherited' from his father, who had been born two days before Trafalgar: Sir Philip Magnus, *Kitchener: Portrait of an Imperialist* (Harmondsworth, 1968), pp. 15–16. I have referred elsewhere to the fusion of two heroes in Mandela's acquisition of the name of Nelson: John M. MacKenzie, 'Nelson goes global: the Nelson myth in Britain and beyond', in David Cannadine (ed.), *Admiral Lord Nelson: Context and Legacy* (London, 2005), pp. 144–65, at p. 147.

[2] John M. MacKenzie, *Propaganda and Empire* (Manchester, 1984); id., *The Empire of Nature* (Manchester, 1988); id., 'Heroic myths of Empire', in id. (ed.), *Popular Imperialism and the Military 1850–1950* (Manchester, 1992), pp. 109–38; id., 'David Livingstone: the construction of the myth', in Graham Walker and Tom Gallagher (eds), *Sermons and Battle Hymns: Protestant Popular Culture in Modern Scotland* (Edinburgh, 1990), pp. 24–42; id., 'David Livingstone and the worldly after-life: imperialism and nationalism in Africa', in id. (ed.), *David Livingstone and the Victorian Encounter with Africa* (London, 1996), pp. 201–17; id., 'T. E. Lawrence: the myth and the message', in Robert Giddings (ed.), *Literature and Imperialism* (London, 1991), pp. 150–81; id., 'The iconography of the exemplary life: the case of David Livingstone', in Geoffrey Cubitt and Allen Warren (eds), *Heroic Reputations and Exemplary Lives* (Manchester, 2000), pp. 84–104; and id., 'Nelson goes global'.

enon and certain key characteristics emerge.[3] Archetypal heroes invariably struggle with cosmic powers of evil, both in terms of individual identity and in the collective psyches of societies. They occupy a vital place in mental representations of the world and satisfy, in the words of the anthropologist Mary Douglas, 'a yearning for rigidity, clear lines, hard concepts'.[4] In all of this, the body of the hero, and what happens to it in its trajectory towards heroic martyrdom, is central. Nelson's body was of course maimed and damaged and that is a potent part of his image. But there is also the question of his dead body. Almost three months elapsed between his death and the funeral in St Paul's Cathedral. In David Livingstone's case, the period was almost a year between his death in 1873 in Central Africa and his funeral in Westminster Abbey in 1874. Gordon's body was never found at all, which lent it an additional significance. All heroes cross a threshold into a fabulous world, an apotheosis occurring after all manner of trials. Nelson and all the imperial heroes seem to follow this pattern, and the magnificent funeral in St Paul's represents this extraordinary passage into mythic status, into a heroic grandeur so central to English-speaking identity that it continues to be celebrated two hundred years later.

Nation states require such myths in order to personify and symbolize state and people. Dominant powers seem to elevate legendary figures as both potent emblems and justifications of the national morality which allegedly underpins and sanctifies their dominance.[5] Of course there is nothing new in all of this. The world of earlier times is littered with such myths, historic figures who epitomized an age or changed the course of history: one thinks of the many mythic recreations of Alexander the Great, Jesus Christ, Mohammed, Cleopatra, Joan of Arc. But what the myths of the nineteenth century, particularly as developed in Victorian times, seem to have in common is the extent to which they were built upon figures who can be located in the middling order of social classes. Scotland's mythic figures have been much commented upon and it is striking to contrast William Wallace, who was from what might be described as the gentry, and Robert the Bruce, who was more aristocratic. The Wallace story has always been more influential and was particularly taken up in the nineteenth

---

[3] See, for example, Sander Gilman, *Difference and Pathology: Stereotypes of Sexuality, Race and Madness* (Ithaca, NY, 1985); Joseph Campbell, *The Hero with a Thousand Faces* (Princeton, 1949); Joseph Henderson, 'Ancient myths and modern man', in Carl G. Jung (ed.), *Man and His Symbols* (London, 1964).

[4] Quoted in Gilman, *Difference and Pathology*, p. 17.

[5] From a vast literature on heroes, see Jenni Calder, *Heroes: From Byron to Guevara* (London, 1977); Graham Dawson, *Soldier Heroes: British Adventure, Empire and the Imagining of Masculinities* (London, 1994); Robert A. Segal, Otto Rank, Lord Raglan, and Alan Dundes, *In Quest of the Hero: The Myth and Birth of the Hero* (Princeton, NJ, 1990).

century, not to mention twentieth-century film. When we reach the age of eighteenth-century empire, General Wolfe emerges as a major hero. As Nicholas Rogers has pointed out, Wolfe was always viewed as a member of the middle class in an age of aristocratic dominance of the army.[6] According to Rogers, his first biographer, John Pringle in 1760, depicted him as 'a paragon of bourgeois rectitude'. Moreover, his death on the Heights of Abraham generated an entire tradition of mythic scenes of heroic death, in which history painters began to find suitably powerful historic moments in contemporary times. As it happens, Wolfe was Nelson's hero. David Livingstone, on the other hand, was from working-class origins but moved into the middle classes through his education, his achievements, and his energizing prescriptions and slogans for missionary, humanitarian, and economic activities. The heroes of the so-called Indian Mutiny were resolutely bourgeois figures, as was 'Chinese' Charles Gordon, whose curious blend of religiosity and militarism (which had been shared by Havelock) appealed greatly to the late Victorian mentality.

If the concept of the bourgeois may be problematic in constructions of social class in the eighteenth century, there can be no doubt that it is fully recognizable in the nineteenth. However much Nelson's vanity was flattered by the titles (not least the Sicilian dukedom) that seemed to propel him up the social scale, his origins in a Norfolk parsonage marked him down as representative of the middle orders, who often achieved social advance through a Royal Navy officer class that was less aristocratic than the army. On his father's side his forebears had been in the church or in trade. He was certainly better connected on his mother's, but even those connections, the Sucklings and the Walpoles, so valuable in his career, were generally from a class identifiably below the truly aristocratic. Socially mobile as he was, and greatly desired to be, by the time that the Nelson cult was greatly developed in Victorian times and appropriated by that age, his upbringing in a Church of England rectory became a positive advantage.[7] It seemed that the bourgeois hero perfectly chimed with the great march

[6] Nicholas Rogers, 'Brave Wolfe: the making of a hero', in Kathleen Wilson (ed.), *A New Imperial History: Culture, Identity and Modernity in Britain and the Empire, 1660–1840* (Cambridge, 2004), pp. 239–59.

[7] C. I. Hamilton, 'Naval hagiography and the Victorian hero', *The Historical Journal*, 23 (1980), 381–98. See also Olive Anderson, 'The growth of Christian militarism in mid-Victorian Britain', *English Historical Review*, 86 (1971), 46–72; Huw Lewis-Jones, ' "Displaying Nelson": navalism and "The Exhibition" of 1891', *The Trafalgar Chronicle*, 14 (2004), 53–86; Andrew Lambert, 'Making a Victorian Nelson: Albert, Nicolas and the arts', *The Trafalgar Chronicle*, 15 (2005), 192–216; and other articles in the same issue by Tim Fulford, Marianne Czisnik, and Huw Lewis-Jones.

of the bourgeoisie in that period, with Victoria's creation of a middle-class monarchy, and with the whole Smilesian philosophy of Self Help.

The bourgeois hero was one with whom the populace could much more readily identify. Of this the Nelson reputation offers a useful representation, although if the cult associated with Nelson has always been greater than that of Wellington this was due to at least three reasons. First, Nelson died in his greatest hour, always a useful means of propelling heroic status, as he himself well knew. Secondly, Nelson's touch was not only naval: he was famously sympathetic towards his sailors in a way that Wellington never was vis-à-vis his soldiers. Thirdly, the navy always had a more patriotic resonance for the British. It was the senior service which, particularly in Victorian times, came to symbolize the perceived greatness of Britain and her Empire. And that brings me to my point of contact with Livingstone, Havelock, and Gordon. Nelson was indeed a genuinely imperial hero, a dimension which has too often been under-emphasized. Nelson, after all, had served in the Arctic, in India, in the Caribbean (where he had married and where Nelson associations and commemorations are celebrated to this day), and in Canada, as well as visiting the Cape (while it was still Dutch). The Battle of Aboukir Bay or the Nile was seen as saving, or at least protecting, India for the British Empire, preparing him for the later actions which would save Britain and, for some, Europe, at least in a supposedly acceptable ideological and geopolitical form.

In my Nelson lecture in London on Trafalgar Day in 2004, I explored the role of the Nelson myth in binding Scots into the Union and in the creation of the 'British World' through imperial guide books as well as through the commemorations that took place in the dominions, notably in Australia and New Zealand.[8] I also pointed out the connections between the cult of Nelson and the emergence of Admiral Togo in Japan as a major hero of rising Japanese power, particularly after the Battle of Tsushima in 1905.[9] Here I want to argue that Canada should have a special space in any consideration of Nelson's legendary status.[10] Nelson served there in 1782, enjoying the excellent climate of Quebec in September and October, which helped to restore his health. He also, briefly, fell in love. It was probably while he was there that he came to idolize Wolfe and, eventually,

---

[8] MacKenzie, 'Nelson goes global'.

[9] This was further developed in John B. Hattendorf, 'Nelson afloat: a hero among the world's navies', in Cannadine (ed.), *Admiral Lord Nelson*, pp. 166–92, particularly at pp. 180 and 182. As Yorimitsu Hashimoto has pointed out to me, there are a number of possible translations of Togo's signal at Tsushima. That he was placing himself in the 'apostolic succession' of the Nelson myth is without doubt.

[10] Nelson's Canadian interlude is usually passed over briefly by his biographers. See, for example, Andrew Lambert, *Nelson: Britannia's God of War* (London, 2004), p. 13.

greatly admire the painting of Wolfe's death scene by Benjamin West, an apotheosis which he hoped to emulate. Quebec had of course been acquired by the British from the French in that key turning-point year of 1759. Its French population, inevitably, had divided loyalties during the French participation in the American War of Independence and the Napoleonic wars, although it was rapidly diluted by immigrants from the British Isles, notably in Montreal, where a very powerful merchant class emerged. The proximity of the Canadian colonies to the United States of America, a potential enemy as in the War of 1812–14, ensured that the Canadians had a special interest in the maintenance of British sea power. This was heightened by the collective memory of the French imperial presence not only in Quebec, but also in Nova Scotia, Cape Breton, and elsewhere in the Gulf of St Lawrence.

In 1905, Canada could hardly fail to celebrate the Trafalgar centenary as fulsomely as possible. The great naval bases at Halifax and Esquimalt were key strategic posts in the British imperial network, while the security of the Atlantic was vital to her commercial survival. Two days before Trafalgar Day, *The Globe*, the Toronto newspaper, published Alfred Austin's poem 'Wardens of the Wave', reprinted from the Trafalgar centenary edition of *The Times* which appeared in London on that date.[11] *The Globe* itself published a magazine supplement on the 21st, while the banner of the main newspaper was made up of the flags of Nelson's famous signal.[12] The editorial for that day expatiated on Britain's illustrious list of naval and military heroes, greater than that of any other nation, with Nelson of course at the top. He was 'endowed with personal qualities which were well calculated to make him a nation's favourite', while his 'winning personality' made him attractive to all. He had made Wellington's achievements possible, and, unlike the Iron Duke, he had enjoyed the love of his men. Thus, Nelson's sexual activities were entirely ignored, as they seem to have been throughout Canada. Whereas there had been some jarring notes in the Australian commemorations, in Canada Emma was conveniently passed over. In Victoria, the Archbishop of Melbourne and Bishop Langley preaching in Bendigo had both spoken of Nelson's moral failings, the latter even dubbing him a 'libertine'.[13] But in Canada, a veil was drawn. He was rather described as having character traits of duty and honour that should be followed by all.

---

[11] *The Globe*, 19 October 1905.

[12] *The Globe*, 21 October 1905. The special supplement of that date contained reproductions of several of the most celebrated Nelson paintings as well as accounts of Trafalgar and its aftermath.

[13] *The Argus*, 23 October 1905.

The accounts of the centenary in this and other Canadian papers were replete with 'examples of noble patriotism', while Nelson was credited with the 'diffusion of truth, liberty and righteousness in all lands'. The fact that Trafalgar Day fell on a Saturday that year clearly helped to ensure that commemorations were well attended throughout the Dominion. In Ottawa a large concourse of school pupils, Normal School students, and many others heard an address by the Governor General, Earl Grey, in which he extolled Nelson's deeds as winning rights and liberties for both the Empire and Europe and as demonstrating that war could be not between nations, but between freedom and despotism, actions devoted to the promotion of self-government over autocracy.[14] He urged his audience to love Nelson, to allow his personality to enter into their lives, and to remember that news of his death had caused strong men to weep. To loud cheers, he proposed that each boy, helped by each girl, should strive to be the Nelson of their generation. Never had any man so entirely possessed the love of his fellow countrymen. R. L. Borden, the future Prime Minister, trusted that all those present would follow his dying words, 'Thank God I have done my duty.' It is intriguing that the commemorative wreaths in Ottawa were laid at the monument to Queen Victoria. Nelson had indeed been appropriated as a Victorian hero. One of the wreaths was made up of Canadian maple leaves, neatly symbolizing the adoption of the hero as an essential part of Canadian identity.

In Hamilton, Ontario, the Premier of the province, Whitney, suggested in his speech that 'Nelson's life had greater results than the life of any other man since the Saviour's time.' The Nelson legend seems frequently to have prompted such striking hyperbole. In Montreal, it was claimed that English- and French-speakers gathered together to honour Nelson, and similar speeches were delivered at the Nelson monument in the Place Jacques-Cartier, a monument erected in 1809 by a group of prominent Montrealers, including influential Scots in that city.[15] Montreal also boasted a Trafalgar Tower, which had been built on private land. It originally had a crenellated top from which a small cannon was fired each year on 21 October. Thus, given the particular demographic make-up of Canada, Nelson was promoted as a hero who had the power to unite the English- and French-speaking populations, particularly in the aftermath of the Entente. But this

---

[14] The account of Grey's speech, together with other speeches in Ottawa and elsewhere in Ontario and the Dominion can be found in *The Globe*, 23 October 1905. See also the *Evening Telegram* of the same date. The newspapers were replete with commercial advertisements in which companies associated their products with the name of Nelson.

[15] I am grateful to Toronto Public Libraries for information about the two Nelson monuments in Montreal.

was not the only diplomatic alliance sanctified by Nelson. On the very day, Monday 23 October, that *The Globe* carried accounts of the Trafalgar Day celebrations across the Dominion, it also described Admiral Togo's victorious entry into Tokyo and his reception by the populace and the Emperor as a great naval hero. The connection between Trafalgar and Tsushima, between Nelson and Togo, was somehow sanctified by this chance conjunction of dates. Togo was from the Satsuma Samurai clan, which made him minor nobility, although he would also have been closely associated with the Meiji Restoration of 1868 and the rapid modernization of Japan that followed. He was virtually deified after this victory and a grand shrine was erected to him in Tokyo. The taking on of this western style of elevating and commemorating heroes as emblems of state power is a striking example of Japanese modernization.

But the twentieth century found a new way of developing myths and of creating, in effect, memorials—no longer in stone, pigment on canvas, or printed engravings, but on celluloid. With the dawning of the age of the popular film, myth-making found a medium which had even more popular resonances than any of its predecessors. It has frequently been objected to me that people walk past statues and memorials in their thousands without giving the person commemorated or their import a second thought. That may be partially true, but with the age of film and, in particular, the development of its immense popularity in the inter-war years—notably with the talkies in the 1930s—audiences encountered myth-making machines as never before, and ones likely to be a good deal more memorable than the speeches of politicians and governors general. The cinema became, in A. J. P. Taylor's words 'the essential social habit of the age'.[16] Radio, in its didactic, improving Reithian guise, was a significant patriotic medium, certainly devoted to the projection of imperial values to the public.[17] But while television as a popular medium had to wait several more decades, it was films that gripped the attention. This is perhaps indicative of the notion that visual media have always had more potency than aural or print ones. A picture, as they say, is worth a thousand words. The statistics of cinema-going in Britain are certainly striking. In 1934, 903 million tickets were sold, rising to 990 million in 1939, and over a billion during the Second World War. Through this period various social surveys, such as Mass

---

[16] Quoted in Jeffrey Richards, *The Age of the Dream Palace: Cinema and Society in Britain 1930–39* (London, 1984), p. 11. The statistics that follow are from the same source, pp. 11–12.
[17] John M. MacKenzie, ' "In Touch with the Infinite": the BBC and the Empire 1923–53', in id. (ed.), *Imperialism and Popular Culture* (Manchester, 1988), pp. 165–91; id., 'Propaganda and the BBC Empire Service, 1932–42', in Jeremy Hawthorn (ed.), *Propaganda, Persuasion, Polemic* (London, 1987), pp. 37–54.

Observation,[18] acknowledged the extraordinary significance of film in influencing public attitudes, while the cinema companies themselves sought to provide ever more striking architectural and design experiences in which the fantasies of films could be presented. We must also remember that this was a truly international medium: the films I am analysing would have been seen not only throughout the United States and the dominions of Canada, South Africa, Australia, and New Zealand, but also in many other territories of the British Empire and—in parallel-language, dubbed or subtitled versions—in Europe.

Just as artists had sought to exploit mythic events in history paintings, so were film-makers on the lookout for epic moments that could be translated into the dramatic medium of the moving picture. In this respect, Nelson was the ideal subject. The reason for this was the presence of a central female character. Whereas in the nineteenth century there had been a real attempt to suppress the Emma Hamilton part of the story, with all its alarming overtones of unbridled passion, adultery, and the breaking of marriage vows, in the twentieth this became the central fascination of dramatization in film. Momentous historical events could be provided with a foreground of a great love affair, even a *ménage à trois* that became, in effect, instrumental in the final trajectory of Nelson's meteoric ascent to his status as the supreme national hero. Emma could come out of her Victorian wraps, as it were, into the twentieth-century spotlight, though not without some difficulties, as we shall see. In this respect, Nelson had a distinct advantage over other nineteenth-century heroes. Although David Livingstone was a prolific father when he had the opportunity, his story was an essentially solitary one. His heroism was precisely founded on the fact that he pursued his greatest achievements as a European alone, albeit with notable African followers. Livingstone featured in a rather earnest educational and religious documentary in 1925. In 1939, Hollywood produced *Stanley and Livingstone*, a film clearly designed to demonstrate the potential power of Anglo-American cooperation. This film had only a tenuous grip upon authenticity, projecting Stanley in the unlikely guise of the amiable Spencer Tracy and Livingstone in the even more unlikely form of the straight-backed English gentleman Cedric Hardwicke. (Hardwicke, incidentally, also played Nelson in a British film of 1926.) More modern films, such as *Lawrence of Arabia*, with the unlikely but effective Peter O'Toole, or *Khartoum*, with Charlton Heston, have failed to solve the signal problem of these heroic myths, the absence of women.

---

[18] Jeffrey Richards and Dorothy Sheridan (eds), *Mass-Observation at the Movies* (London and New York, 1987).

No such problem confronted those seeking to bring Nelson to the screen. Here the momentous tale of national survival, with all its overtones of identity formation in the face of the hostile and dangerous European Other, could be given a cast of central female roles—Emma of course, but also her mother, the Queen of Naples, and Lady Nelson—to match Nelson, Hardy, Sir William Hamilton, Earl Spencer (First Lord of the Admiralty), and the Revd Edmund, Nelson's father. A powerful personal story, stranger than any fiction, could be counterpointed with what were, in effect, world events. The navy has always had powerful sexual overtones. The well-known phrases tell it all: 'All the nice girls love a sailor', or 'A girl in every port.' Not to mention the images of testosterone-fuelled sailors on the beach, whether in the South Seas or in the taverns and brothels of every naval port. I am not here laying aside moral, gender, or racial sensitivities. I am merely pointing up traditional representations in popular culture, in the theatre, and in travel narratives into which the Nelson story could perfectly fit. Nelson provided a louche smirk of recognition as well as the notion that great men have to be excused the foibles, the excesses even, of the landward contrast to shipboard asceticism. Lord Spencer himself makes the point in *That Hamilton Woman*, a film which I shall consider further below, when he says 'Only the weaknesses of the great are glaring.'

The Nelson story was also, of course, particularly potent at time of war, a period of heightened dangers in which the social and sexual conventions of peace are swept up into the violence and anxieties of conflict. It is therefore no surprise that the first film on the subject, with the simple title *Nelson*, was conceived during the First World War, shot in 1918 and released just after the war ended. It has been described as a 'lavish and spectacular epic', designed as an educational and propagandist tool, presenting the inspirational Nelson as the ideal national type.[19] Nelson is portrayed as a hero who overcomes all adversities and bodily weaknesses to triumph. Nelson's England is represented in idyllic and idealized form, contrasting with the exotic backdrops against which he has to play out his noble endeavours. The narrative technique used in this age of the silent film is of a retired admiral telling the story to a boy through 'inter-titles' so lengthy that they would not have been tolerated in other types of film. This device also perfectly fits the contention that heroic myths are powerfully designed for the instruction of youth, the passing on of national mores to each new generation. But the makers of the film faced a real dilemma when they were overtaken by peace. The film had been conceived as an exercise in wartime propaganda, in which the French of the past stood in for the

[19] Karel Dibbets and Bert Hogenkamp, *Film and the First World War* (Amsterdam, 1995), pp. 108–15.

74

Germans of the present. With the war over, it had to be marketed as a blend of national epic with stirring personal story. Emma could not now be avoided, but her story could be portrayed as that of the temptation which the hero overcomes. Tempted as he is by her voracious charms, duty and responsibility to the nation always triumph. Domestic scenes could be inter-cut with grand representational images of world-changing events in which the needs of the latter always take precedence, culminating in the intimacy and masculinity of the death scene.

It was clear to film-makers that this story was a winner. Further British films, now always foregrounding Emma Hamilton, followed in 1919, 1926, and 1973. The Germans produced Hamilton films in 1921 and 1969, while Hollywood participated in 1929 and 1941 (though this famous film, *Lady Hamilton*, was essentially British). It is a curious fact that in the 1920s the German cinema began to be intrigued by British literary and historical myths. That baleful icon of German film acting of the period, Conrad Veidt, appeared in the dual roles in Robert Louis Stevenson's *Dr Jekyll and Mr Hyde* in 1920. In the following year, Veidt graduated to that other dual role, Admiral Nelson and Horatio the Lover.[20] It has been said that Veidt appreciated having a romantic lead to play rather than his usual demoni-acal figure, but a still of him as Nelson, dark-eyed and scowling, gives the viewer the distinct sensation that one would not like to meet him on a darkened quarter-deck. In short, Veidt's Nelson looks more Conrad than Horatio. But this film went beyond its earlier British counterpart by bring-ing Lady Hamilton fully downstage. It was even called *Lady Hamilton* or *The Affairs of Lady Hamilton*, and it may be that the Germans wished to convey the idea that this greatest of all British heroes was flawed by his sexual susceptibilities.

Intriguingly, there was a later German version, based on an Alexandre Dumas take on the Nelson story.[21] Entitled *Lady Hamilton—zwischen Schmach und Liebe* (*Between Ignominy and Love*), it took Dumas's inevitably hostile view of Nelson and the British. To explain, Dumas spent some time in Naples editing a newspaper sympathetic to the cause of the Risorgimento and at the same time researched a three-volume history of the Neapolitan Bourbons.[22] In the course of this research, he became intrigued by the Nelson–Hamilton story and published his own version of the love story in the early 1860s, *La San Felice*. This novel was very popular in France but was

---

[20] Jerry C. Allen, *Conrad Veidt: From Caligari to Casablanca* (Pacific Grove, Calif., 1987), pp. 53–4.

[21] *Monthly Film Bulletin*, 36 (December 1969), 267–8.

[22] Frederick W. J. Hemmings, *The King of Romance: A Portrait of Alexandre Dumas* (London, 1979), p. 198.

published in English, in what has been described as a 'cruelly abridged version', as *The Lovely Lady Hamilton* or *The Beauty and the Glory* in 1903. Though the film was German, it had a French director, some English actors, and also had an English-language version. It was released in 1968 and was clearly designed to counterpoint English prudery with British historic successes. It was given an X certificate, and has been described as featuring more na*vel* than na*val* encounters. It hinted at a Lesbian relationship between Emma and the Queen of Naples, while its climax features a heart-broken Emma and Nelson's daughter Horatia being refused entry to St Paul's for the state funeral. The film could be interpreted as indicating that the British were unworthy of their heroes. They failed to honour Nelson's dying wish and heartlessly denied Emma both her honour and her rewards. Moral sanctimoniousness triumphed over fidelity to the hero's wishes.

But with *Lady Hamilton* (US title *That Hamilton Woman*, by which it is now more commonly known), we arrive at the most celebrated Nelson–Hamilton film.[23] It was conceived by that most patriotically British of Hungarians, Alexander Korda, and it is possible that Korda was encouraged in his propagandist ends by both Robert Vansittart (the anti-appeasement former permanent under-secretary at the Foreign Office) and Winston Churchill. Churchill, indeed, came to see it as his favourite film and insisted on repeated viewings during the war. I am sure that Churchill saw himself in the role of Nelson, saving the nation, and one scene in particular, where Emma invites Nelson onto a hotel balcony to acknowledge the cheering crowds below, has a distinctly Churchillian look. Korda went to the United States to shoot it in late 1940 and the entire film was put together with extraordinary speed in the space of six weeks. Like most of the other films, the naval actions are supplied by models in tanks—always a problem in any representation of Nelson's heroic moments. The leads were famously taken by Vivien Leigh and Laurence Olivier and the film therefore had the additional frisson of their off-screen relationship. To say that neither was particularly suitable would be something of an understatement. Leigh has a cut-glass accent and peerless looks. While Emma became increasingly fat and frumpish, which left some wondering where the attraction lay, Leigh remains divinely svelte throughout, capable of acts of athleticism as she runs through villas, along vast balconies, and across hotel rooms. And while Leigh is too thin, Olivier is too large. Sensitive though his portrayal is in some respects, he could not convey the slight physical fragility of the real and maimed Nelson. His acting has indeed been described as 'passionless

[23] Karol Kuelik, *Alexander Korda: The Man who Could Work Miracles* (London, 1975), pp. 245–55, provides an account of the making of this film. I do not always agree with this author's judgement on aspects of the quality and content of the film.

and stagey', though public and critics enjoyed the iconic death scene. Korda clearly had no moral anxieties about the story. Emma is delivered as a heroine in her own right, acting as the effective go-between from Nelson to the Queen of Naples (the true King as it says in the film), outflanking her husband and entitling her to be regarded, in her turn, as the true ambassador. She also nurses Nelson in his illness and exhaustion, restoring him to health for future actions. Thus she is not only enthralled by the glory of Nelson; she is actively instrumental in its creation. By contrast, Lady Nelson, who appears in the later scenes of the film when the Hamilton–Nelson threesome have returned to London, is portrayed as an unbending, hard-hearted, and thoroughly unsympathetic figure who would be likely to drive anyone into the arms of Emma. Yet the film is framed by Emma's degradation in a debtors' prison in Calais, a device that permits Korda to give her the narrative voice as she tells a fellow English inmate of her stirring past before drink and money troubles caught up with her. It seems to me that this is profoundly ambivalent. There can be no doubt that Korda places her in a heroic role and her fate therefore bespeaks establishment ingratitude. Yet some might also take it as representing the wages of sin.

The film is, of course, freighted with contemporary concerns. There are a number of references to the British Empire, to Napoleon's designs upon India, to the successful wars of the eighteenth century, to Clive of India, and the dangers to Britain's global role. The central propagandist moment comes with Nelson's speech to the Lords of the Admiralty in opposition to the Peace of Amiens, in which he argues that Napoleon is not to be appeased (though the word is not used), that he is only gaining time before the war will be resumed with alliances designed to destroy the British Empire, that he means to be master of the world, and that dictators must be wiped out and destroyed. The contemporary resonance could not be clearer to any member of the audience.

But Emma's fate did not satisfy the Hollywood censor, and the American political establishment was distinctly uneasy with its political message. The film appeared to the censor to be condoning adultery and Korda was forced to include an extra scene in which Nelson's father upbraided him and the hero admitted his error. Korda was never happy with this and most of the scene was later cut. Worse, an isolationist Senate investigation committee was convinced that Hollywood had become a nest of British propagandists and was in the act of summoning various producers and directors before it. Chaplin was already in trouble for *The Great Dictator* and Korda was summoned to give an account of his shameless anti-German propaganda. A matter of days before Korda's scheduled appearance, the Japanese attacked Pearl Harbor and the matter was dropped. The 'land of the free' had been saved from some ludicrous Senate posturing. There is little doubt that the anti-British propaganda investigations were eventually to turn into the un-American activities witch-hunt, which would again implicate Chaplin. Mercifully, these acts of isolationist and ideological narrow-mindedness had no effect upon the popularity of these films. *That Hamilton Woman*, in Britain more demurely *Lady Hamilton*, was a smash hit, not only in the English-speaking world but also in such unlikely areas as Russia and South America.

The final Nelson portrayal leads us to Terence Rattigan. In 1964 he was invited by Associated Television to cooperate in the transmission of three plays, one of which was to be specially commissioned.[24] The Duke of Edinburgh was to introduce the latter and the proceeds were to go to his Awards Scheme and to the preservation of the *Cutty Sark*. Rattigan thought initially of Nelson, but he usually preferred to write about failures, not success stories. But the Duke of Edinburgh pointed out to him that Nelson's great defeat had been his failure to get the nation to accept Emma. Rattigan set about writing a play in which Emma was portrayed in a hostile way, as 'an absolute cow', as he put it himself. In *That Hamilton Woman* Nelson's stepson Josiah Nisbet supposedly provides the title phrase in a letter to his mother. In Rattigan's version the conflict between Nelson's public and private life would be similarly narrated by a mystified, hero-worshipping Nelson nephew. In 1972 the play, scarcely adapted at all, was translated into a film funded by Hollywood but made in Britain by James Cellan Jones, now entitled *Bequest to the Nation*. The money did not extend to decent battle scenes and those that had appeared in the earlier film *Captain Horatio Hornblower RN* of 1950 were simply reused: this cheapened the film rather noticeably since the colour quality was completely different. Peter Finch was Nelson and Glenda Jackson appeared as Emma, by her own admission badly miscast. Rattigan's comments on her performance were rather more than mildly abusive. He suggested that Jackson had left a lot out, such as Hamilton's love for Nelson, 'which is quite important. She played her as a mean-spirited bitch, instead of a great-hearted whore, but I suppose that is her range.'[25] Nelson appeared now to be in second place, though the film and the play on which it was based made only a slight impact, after Rattigan, typically, had made a great deal of money. In many respects these successive depictions of the Nelson–Emma story epitomize the developing moral mood of the twentieth century and its contrasts with the nineteenth.

By contrast, the composer Lennox Berkeley must have made very little out of his efforts to create a Nelson opera. Intriguingly, it was probably

---

[24] Michael Darlow and Gillian Hodson, *Terence Rattigan: The Man and His Work* (London, 1979), pp. 276–89.

[25] Quoted in Darlow and Hodson, *Terence Rattigan*, p. 289.

commissioned for performance in 1951, the year of the Festival of Britain, when British identity was being reforged in a more national and less imperial form. In the event, the opera was not completed until 1954, when it was performed at Sadler's Wells in London. A substantial opera in three acts, it was probably Berkeley's most notable excursion into operatic form. But of course there were problems. It was somewhat static and it lacked battle scenes. It has never been revived, although concert performances have indicated that it was a major work with much to commend it.[26]

The bicentenary of Trafalgar stimulated some new musical expressions. The distinguished soprano Catherine Bott gave numerous performances of her specially devised entertainment based on Lady Hamilton's Songbooks, and on Trafalgar Day itself she was the soloist in the world premiere of a Nelson cantata commissioned from the composer Errollyn Wallen for BBC Radio 3 — a latter-day echo of Joseph Haydn's famous Nelson Mass.

Music of this sort is perhaps more elusive and elitist, but the cinematic narratives had contrived to take national icons which had been frozen in stone, pigment, or print engravings and provide them with flesh and blood again. Nelson's death scene, as recreated by artists, had certainly been portrayed on countless stages in that favourite Victorian spectacle, the *tableau vivant*. Now he was impersonated by actors who moved and talked, projected by the most exciting new medium of the age. It seems to me that an essentially demotic medium took him up as a man, and therefore a great hero, of the people. His sailors love him (in *That Hamilton Woman* they sing songs that sound as though they are being performed by a very fine Welsh male-voice choir) in return for his celebrated care for them. His famous signal strikes a powerful chord within them.

But although he had come to epitomize national heroism on the grandest scale, Nelson was physically and socially a little man who had performed the largest of deeds. Though he had arrived at a viscountcy and a Sicilian dukedom, the audience had to be reminded of his relatively lowly origins. The Revd Edmund Nelson describes himself in *That Hamilton Woman* as a 'humble country parson' who deals with simple people who 'fight in the depths of their souls the same temptations as you' (his son). Part of the message of the national myth, which helped to make it potent throughout the British Empire, was that Nelson was a simple middle-class hero who, on his ships, had lived close to ordinary people. He supposedly lacked aristocratic airs and graces, unlike Wellington, and his transparent pleasure and personal vanity in respect of his social advancement could be overlaid by his supposed feeling for ordinary folk. The point about the

---

[26] Amanda Holden (ed.), *The Viking Opera Guide* (London, 1993), p. 90.

Victorian hailing of middle- or working-class heroes is that, in a real sense, they had to make themselves before their handling of events gave them their heroic auras. That was why they were so widely appreciated in the homilies of the churches, the textbooks of educators, the theatrical presentations of impresarios, the propaganda of politicians, and the plot lines of popular fiction. They were supposedly figures with whom the great majority of the population could identify themselves.[27] They were very human individuals who became superhuman national icons. If Nelson saved the nation, the grandest sacrifice of all, Havelock and his fellow 'Mutiny' heroes saved the Indian Empire (as Nelson had done before them), Livingstone saved Africa by liberating it from the Arab slave trade and from superstition, while Gordon ultimately saved both China and the vast lands of the upper Nile Valley from fanaticism. This is, of course, the way it would have been put by their hagiographers. These heroes were the saviours of the nation and the Empire, the redeemers of past failings, the defenders of fundamental values, the manufacturers of a new national identity, and with it an inspirational destiny. They provided a heroic touchstone for the future, sanctified by martyrdom. They epitomized the mythic status which was transmitted through the development of print capitalism and of many entertainment and artistic forms, filtered by a distinctive Victorian approach to their legendary status. Thus Nelson was bourgeois, national, and imperial, lending him international significance. This was the kind of myth much valued by the Victorians and it was they, in many ways, who transmitted it forward into the twentieth and twenty-first centuries. There it was taken up by wholly new media, notably the cinema. And, as we have seen, cinematic treatment both broadened, and in some respects cheapened, the power of the Nelson and other myths, bringing them to a much wider global public.

Note. I am deeply grateful to my friend and colleague Professor Jeffrey Richards, my Toronto cousins Rosemarie and Robert Spearpoint, my postgraduate student Yorimitsu Hashimoto, and the singer Catherine Bott for some of the information on which this paper is based. The interpretative frame is provided by myself and I am consequently responsible for any errors.

[27] I take a different line, more closely associated with popular culture, from that of Andrew Lambert, *Nelson: Britannia's God of War*, ch. 17, 'Nelson revived 1885–2005', where the focus is much more on questions of high naval and defence policy. I would argue that it was the lodging of the Nelson myth in the popular consciousness that permits pressure groups and policy-makers to invoke his name in their cause, with popular support.

II
Bicentenary 2005

5.
Trafalgar: Back on the Map of British Popular Culture? Assessing the 2005 Bicentenary

MARK CONNELLY

Introduction

During 2005 I witnessed and monitored various commemorative events with the intention of discovering the current state of knowledge about Nelson, Trafalgar, and Britain's maritime history and future, and to explore whether the events had helped to raise public awareness of these issues. Various methodological problems were thrown up by this task. Using the media to assess public attitudes and knowledge is fraught with difficulty. Newspapers, radio, and television reports and features might take a particular stance, but it is impossible to know whether their readers, listeners, and viewers found such approaches acceptable, important, and reliable. The same is true of public events and exhibitions. No matter how carefully designed, constructed, and stage-managed, it remains extremely hard to judge impact precisely. Partly in order to overcome this difficulty, and in order to gain a direct 'popular' voice into the study, various interviews were conducted. The interviews were concentrated into three periods and aimed at particular audiences. The first set was conducted in Portsmouth between 28 and 29 June during the International Fleet Review. The second was held a week later in the Simon Langton Grammar School for Boys in Canterbury with a range of boys aged between twelve and fourteen years of age. The final set was among undergraduates currently engaged in the History BA programmes at the University of Kent's School of History in September 2005. The sample was by no means scientifically devised or fully representative of the population. However, it did provide a fair cross-section, and in particular explored the image of Trafalgar among the young, a key audience for the Official Nelson Commemoration Committee (ONCC). Chaired by the eminent naval historian and museologist, Dr Colin White, the ONCC acted as a coordinating and advisory body, and dealt with many different ideas and suggested many events. The youth audience was of particular interest to the ONCC, as there was a perception that this demographic was most unsure of the role of the navy and the sea in British life. By using the media and interviews as an indicator of values, a methodology similar to that deployed by Martin Shaw and Jeffrey Walsh to assess the impact of the Gulf War on Britain was used.[1] The use of this approach allowed Trafalgar to be explored as a *realm of memory*, as defined by Pierre Nora. Nora identified 'dominant and dominated sites of memory' in his investigations. A dominant site is spectacular and imposing, often reflecting the collective will of a clearly identified authority, while the latter, 'dominated' memory, is that placed on a site or event by ordinary participants. Such processes can lead to clashes of interpretation as well as consensus.[2] The year 2005 certainly witnessed much debate between dominant and dominated memory in the landscape of the Trafalgar bicentenary.

Public Awareness before 2005

Popular knowledge of Trafalgar was probably best summed up in the successful 1980s television comedy, *Blackadder*. The third series was set during the Regency, and contained some excellent indicators of public awareness:

> [*The characters discuss the recent General Election and the fact that no one appears to have the right to vote.*]
> BLACKADDER   Because virtually no one is—women, peasants, chimpanzees, lunatics, lords.
> BALDRICK   No, that's not true. Lord Nelson's got a vote.
> BLACKADDER   He's got a *boat*, Baldrick.
> [*Then Blackadder hatches a plan to enter the House of Lords and returns with his new robes.*]
> MRS MIGGINS   Oh, very nice! And it's real cat, isn't it?
> BLACKADDER   This is not cat, Mrs Miggins. It is finest leather-trimmed ermine with gold medallion accessories.
> MRS MIGGINS   Oh, go on, Mr Blackadder, it's cat. Oh, they've left the little collars on!

[1] Martin Shaw, 'Past wars and present conflicts: from the Second World War to the Gulf', and Jeffrey Walsh, 'Remembering Desert Storm: popular culture and the Gulf War', in Martin Evans and Kenneth Lunn (eds), *War and Memory in the Twentieth Century* (Oxford, 1997), pp. 191–204 and pp. 205–22.
[2] Pierre Nora, 'Between memory and history: les lieux de mémoire', *Representations*, 26 (1989), 7–25; id. (ed.), *Realms of Memory: Rethinking the French Past*, 3 vols (New York, 1996), vol. 1, p. xi.

BLACKADDER [*reads a medallion*] 'Mr Friskie. If found please return to Emma Hamilton, Marine Parade, Portsmouth.' Damn! Oh, well. Who cares about a dead cat now that I am a fat cat?

[*In a later episode Blackadder discusses strategy with the Duke of Wellington.*]

BLACKADDER   As I understand it, Napoleon is in North Africa. And Nelson is stationed in . . . ?

WELLINGTON   Alaska, your Highness. In case Boney should trick us by coming via the North Pole.

BLACKADDER   Hmmm. Perhaps a preferable stratagem might be to harry him amid-ships as he leaves the Mediterranean. Let's see—ahm, Trafalgar might be quite a good spot.

WELLINGTON   Trafalgar? Well, I'll mention it to Nelson . . .[3]

As these exchanges show, it might be assumed that the British people had lost touch with the sea, the Royal Navy, and their maritime heroes of history. Knowledge had fallen into a somewhat sketchy state, and was reduced to a few unreliable facts. It is tempting to believe that once upon a time, and not too long ago either, Britons swelled with pride at the names 'Trafalgar', 'Nelson', and 'Victory'. However, in trying to assess the impact of the bicentenary events it was first necessary to remind myself that I was not necessarily measuring a state of low recognition against that of a previous high. Turning to that most essential of British history books, W. C. Sellar and R. J. Yeatman's *1066 and All That*, I found that in 1930 this most 'memorable' tale of British history was construed as follows:

Chapter 47

Nelson

Napoleon ought never to be confused with Nelson, in spite of their hats being so alike; they can most easily be distinguished from one another by the fact that Nelson always stood with his arm *like this*, while Napoleon always stood with his arms *like that*. [There is no accompanying illustration.]

Nelson was one of England's most naval officers, and despised weak commands. At one battle when he was told that his Admiral-in-Chief had ordered him to cease fire, he put the telephone under his blind arm and exclaimed in disgust: 'Kiss me, Hardy!'

By this and other intrepid manoeuvres the French were utterly driven from the seas.[4]

It should also be stated that in Sellar and Yeatman's utterly memorable history there is not one specific mention of Trafalgar, but there are three pages on Wellington, Waterloo, and the 'gorilla war' in Spain.

[3] Richard Curtis, Ben Elton, Rowan Atkinson, and John Lloyd, *Blackadder: The Whole Damn Dynasty, 1485–1917* (Harmondsworth, 1999), pp. 235, 249, 332.

[4] W. C. Sellar and R. J. Yeatman, *1066 and All That* (London, 1930), p. 97.

At the turn of the bicentenary year many influential people, particularly politicians and journalists, were convinced that previous generations of Britons were much more attuned to the significance of Trafalgar than Sellar and Yeatman's statements suggest. An official report into the state of history teaching in British schools, published in December 2004, condemned the over-concentration on the Holocaust and Nazism, and the lack of a British history element in the curriculum, which resulted in widespread ignorance of Britain's past achievements.[5] Early in the New Year the Conservative shadow education secretary, Tim Collins, recorded his dismay that fewer than half of Britain's eleven- to eighteen-year-olds knew the name of Nelson's flagship at the Battle of Trafalgar. He noted his determination to introduce a new curriculum to counteract such ignorance, which he went on to describe as 'an outright scandal'.[6] The right-wing historian Andrew Roberts was asked to chair a panel to advise on a new curriculum, and the *Daily Telegraph* gave it some guidance by suggesting the key importance of Trafalgar in British history: 'Nelson personified the qualities of the Royal Navy in an era when it made Britain feared in every corner of the planet.'[7] Here the right-wing press and right-wing politicians created the parameters that framed the debate for the rest of the year. They treated the perception that the general public, particularly those under thirty years old, were in deep ignorance as to the significance of Trafalgar, Nelson, and the Royal Navy, as a national scandal. As the right-wing media tended to foreground the com-memorations more strongly than the centre-left and left-wing media, its comments also emerged far more strongly. From this point of view, the emotions and concepts underpinning the commemorative year had to be patriotism and pride in order to restore British national identity. Even the curator of the Norfolk Museum, the county of Nelson's birth, stated that '80% of Norfolk "folk" have little idea who Nelson was. Many have *no* idea why there's a museum in Yarmouth or what his links with Norfolk are. Most don't care.'[8] Any deviation from these crucial framing devices was regarded with extreme scepticism; but the chances of one, overarching interpretation of the meaning of 1805 were remote given the number and diversity of organizations involved and events planned.

---

[5] *Daily Telegraph*, 26 December 2004.
[6] Ibid., 27 January 2005.
[7] Ibid.
[8] Letter to the author, 2 March 2005, original emphasis.

Organizing the Bicentenary: Events and Reactions

At the heart of the planning for the bicentenary was the ONCC, and the idea that it could help to flick a Nelson switch deep in the souls of the British people. It revealed a confidence not shared by many right-wing politicians and the right-wing media, which clearly believed in a shameful collapse of knowledge.[9] Study of the plans devised by the various organizations that were involved in commemorating the bicentenary makes it clear that many different agendas could be served by latching on to this significant anniversary. Local museums keen to raise their profile among their communities were given the opportunity to exploit occasionally tenuous links in the search for publicity, profit, and affirmation of their role. The curator of the Norfolk Museum, for example, stated unequivocally that the commemoration was a crucial part of a campaign to raise public awareness of its existence.[10] For the Royal Navy, meanwhile, the year was an excellent opportunity to promote recruitment and its role in the defence of British interests. An official navy publication noted its strategic objectives in the bicentenary celebrations:

- to increase public support and advocacy for the Royal Navy;
- to increase awareness of the importance of the UK maritime sector;
- to increase interest in the Royal Navy as a career opportunity and provide an inspiring experience for serving personnel;
- to promote the inspirational legacy of Nelson for all people;
- to develop international naval links.[11]

Admiral Sir Alan West reiterated these points in an article for the *Sunday Express*, stating that the year was designed to achieve 'a better understanding of our nation's maritime history, the continued importance of the maritime community to Britain's economy and global standing, and the relevance of the role played by today's Royal Navy'.[12]

For the National Trust and the Woodland Trust it was the chance to highlight conservation of British woodland with the main site, Victory Wood in Kent, part of a plan to maintain and restore 'an internationally important concentration of ancient woodland that is one of the last strongholds of the heath fritillary butterfly and home to the increasingly

---

[9] Interview with Colin White, 25 May 2005, and letter to the author from John Graves, Secretary ONCC, 17 March 2005.
[10] Letter to the author, 2 March 2005.
[11] *Broadsheet: Overview of the Year 2003–2004* (London, 2004), p. 30.
[12] *Sunday Express*, 22 October 2005.

rare dormouse'.[13] The year 2005 can thus be seen as a significant platform for the promotion of many different types of cause. It would appear that many of the events used relatively tenuous links with the Nelson and Trafalgar celebrations to promote their ongoing activities. The ONCC itself wanted to stress the role of the sea, Nelson, and the navy in British history, culture, economics, and politics while also emphasizing international fellowship symbolized by humanity's ancient and boundless relationship with the seas and oceans. Whether the ONCC achieved this rather tricky double objective is, again, difficult comprehensively to assess.

The most elaborate element in the Trafalgar 200 celebrations was the Fleet Review and *son et lumière* re-enactment of the battle on 28 June in the Solent. As the largest Fleet Review since 1897, involving ships from thirty-five navies, the sheer organizational effort of the coordinating committees was hugely successful. The evening *son et lumière* was equally complex, involving the choreography of fifteen tall ships and the use of 10,000 fireworks, weighing more than 12 tons, fired from thirty-five pontoons. Advance publicity for the event, particularly in the Portsmouth area, ensured a large turnout, and the crowd was estimated at 250,000.[14] Viewed in these terms the Review must be judged a success. However, close study reveals a range of reactions to the event. Some sections of the media and public perceived it in a resoundingly positive manner. The editorial in *The Times* recorded the enthusiasm of the crowd and took it as a sign 'that Horatio Nelson's magnificent victory at Trafalgar . . . and his death in the hour of victory, are far from being forgotten', and added 'Children still learn of Admiral Nelson's victory over the French and Spanish fleet that ended the threat of invasion by Napoleon Bonaparte and established British naval supremacy for a century.'[15] Similarly impressed was *The News*, Portsmouth's local newspaper, which published a special souvenir edition packed with praise for the event and its organizers. The huge number of visitors was stressed, as was the estimated £60 million spent by the tourists who flooded into the city. The editorial trumpeted: 'What a triumph. What a staggering success. What exhilarating proof that we can put on a show to thrill the world.'[16] Another theme picked out by many sections of the press was the welcome sense of Anglo-French unity that appeared to permeate the event. Vice Admiral Jacques Mazars and the captain of the *Charles de Gaulle*, Xavier Magne, both stressed the willing cooperation of the French navy in the event. *The Times* and the *Daily Telegraph* commented on this and both

---

[13] *Broadleaf: The Magazine of the Woodland Trust*, 64 (Spring 2005), 25.
[14] *Daily Telegraph*, 27 June 2005; *The News* (Portsmouth local newspaper), 29 June 2005.
[15] *The Times*, 29 June 2005.
[16] *The News*, 29 June 2005.

Figure 5.1.   *Broadleaf,* Woodland Trust Magazine, 64 (Spring 2005), cover image. © Getty Images.

recorded, in light-hearted fashion, the playing of 'La Marseillaise' as the Queen sailed past, along with the French officer who, when asked to name a famous French naval victory replied, 'Beeeep! No comment.'[17] In this sense, the atmosphere of the bicentenary coincided neatly with the celebrations that marked the 1905 centenary. As Bertrand Taithe points out in Chapter 3 above, the centenary was commemorated against the background of Anglo-French rapprochement in the wake of the Entente Cordiale. The need to maintain healthy Anglo-French relations created a strange mixture of celebration and joint commemoration, stressing the valour of both sides. In 2005 this similarity of approach was largely forgotten, as many were convinced that in past years Britain would never have been so

[17] *The Times*, 29 June 2005; *Daily Telegraph*, 29 June 2005.

pusillanimous. The prevalence of this feeling in the popular right-wing press shows the ignorance of the way previous commemorations of Trafalgar had been handled, and a misunderstanding of Britain's attitude towards its Continental neighbours even when apparently at the pinnacle of its power and influence.

THE Sun SAYS

Nelson's Day

ADMIRAL Lord Nelson was not just the greatest naval commander ever.

He also single-handedly changed the entire course of European history and established Britain's role as a world power in the 19th and 20th centuries.

So why the heck doesn't Britain shout his praises from the rooftops?

Let's have a Trafalgar Day each year on October 21, the anniversary of his historic defeat of the French and Spanish navies.

Yesterday's Trafalgar celebration, timed to coincide with the Queen's review of the Fleet, was magnificent.

It reminded us of what made this country great and what keeps it that way — the dedication and bravery of the men and women of our Armed Forces.

It was only at the last minute that the BBC overcame its silly political correctness and decided to show live coverage of the event.

We must never be afraid or ashamed to salute our national heroes.

Figure 5.2. *The Sun*, editorial column, 29 June 2005, p. 8. © *The Sun* 2005.

Figure 5.3. Bill Caldwell, *Battle of Trafalgar: Red Team v Blue Team*, cartoon published in *The Sun*, 29 June 2005, p. 8. By courtesy of Bill Caldwell.

Those unimpressed by the 2005 commemorations, and certainly those who were of the opinion that the Britannia of old would never have countenanced anything less than a full-blooded celebration, were the popular right-wing dailies, notably *The Sun* and the *Daily Mail*. Both were especially angry about the decision to play down the Trafalgar element in the *son et lumière* event in favour of a 'red' versus 'blue' naval battle. *The Sun* reported the disappointment of Anna Tribe, Nelson's great-great-great-granddaughter. Her alleged judgement that it was 'Political correctness . . . gone totally mad' suited *The Sun*'s self-proclaimed role as guardian of all that is great about Britain.[18] The *Daily Mail* took a similar line, reminding the 'panjandrums of political correctness that at Trafalgar the Reds did not fight the Blues—the British beat the French, resulting in the creation of

[18] *The Sun*, 29 June 2005.

the greatest navy and arguably most beneficial empire in history.'[19] Further controversy was stirred up by the BBC's lack of coverage. Unable to resist its old enemy, *The Sun* derided the BBC for 'its silly political correctness'.[20] A similar point was made in the *Daily Telegraph*. It reported that viewers had complained to the broadcaster over its lack of coverage, and managed to get a BBC insider to admit that 'perhaps [we] did underestimate the popularity of the event.'[21] Ironically, the newspaper often seen as the mouthpiece of politically correct values, and so one which might have been in sympathy with the supposedly 'lily-livered' version of events, *The Guardian*, was equally unimpressed. Far from seeing the commemorations as marking a more reflective interpretation of the battle, *The Guardian*'s front page carried a reference to Adam Nicolson's article in the G2 section, titled 'Celebrating the carnage of Trafalgar is obscene'. Comparing the devastation of Trafalgar to that of the Somme or Passchendaele, Nicolson expressed his utter incomprehension that such a bloody event could ever be celebrated. He labelled it a failure to understand that the victory was the triumph of a ruthless and utterly unsentimental nation. Perhaps even more condemnatory was the questioning of the participants' credentials: 'What is a Nigerian ship doing there? Or a Serbian? Two from Pakistan? And three from South Korea?'[22] The dark implications of recognizing suspect nations were matched in the editorial which followed up this damning note. Satirizing the Royal Navy's claim that the event was about maritime cooperation, it hinted at outright hypocrisy, and went on to declare:

> Spurning a more cynical explanation for the gathering of the fleets—that, given the usual reluctance by armies and navies to celebrate their defeats, what is actually being celebrated is the idea of war itself—we are left with the conclusion that 200 years is the time taken for blood to cool, and for old wars to turn, in the imagination, from tragic-heroic to quaint-heroic.[23]

Interpreting Public Attitudes

Assessing the attitudes of members of the public who witnessed the event is more problematic. Those unable to attend in person were frustrated by the somewhat unclear attitude to the day of BBC television and ITV

[19] *Daily Mail*, 29 June 2005.
[20] *The Sun*, 29 June 2005.
[21] *Daily Telegraph*, 30 June 2005.
[22] *The Guardian*, G2 section, 28 June 2005.
[23] *The Guardian*, 28 June 2005.

Figure 5.4. Detail from Adam Nicolson, 'Jamboree is no way to celebrate Trafalgar', *The Guardian*, G2 section, 28 June 2005.
© Olivier Kugler 2005.

news.[24] Direct, readily accessible, free-to-air television coverage was rather staccato, and consistent coverage could be found only on the satellite channels. The audiences for the event were therefore largely those who took the time and trouble to track it down. Given this scenario it is unlikely that those unaware of Nelson and the Trafalgar commemorations would have been enlightened by the event. In effect, television coverage preached to the converted. Examining the large crowds at Portsmouth, albeit in a rather unscientific way, and via a number of sources, reveals an ambiguous picture. It should be stated that I stood on the waterfront near Fort Gladstone, which was not on the easily accessible tourist route, and so none of the people I interviewed on the Review day were from outside the Portsmouth area, and all had some connection with the Royal Navy. All, therefore, had a direct reason for wishing to witness the events. It was possible to detect a strong element of local pride in people's reactions. In effect I was told that Portsmouth was showing the world what it was about: the Royal Navy. I was left with the impression that the navy belonged to Portsmouth, and the rest of the country needed to understand that fact.[25] Equally important was the feeling that the history of the Royal Navy and Britain's connection with the sea were missing from children's education. No one was at all interested in taking a politically correct view of the battle re-enactment, although all showed a marked aversion to expressing this too strongly. I took this to be in deference to my academic credentials, which probably made people suspect that I held views of a pronounced 'Guardian type'. A friend of mine told me about two of his workmates who grew up in Portsmouth and whose families worked in the dockyard. They reported their complaints about missing the Review, and the enlightening comment: 'I'm from Pompey, and war's my thing.'[26] The sensation that the event was above all else a celebration of Portsmouth and its local identity was reinforced fully in The News. Comments were reported from eighty-eight spectators, but only fourteen lived more than fifty miles from the city.[27]

The Final Round of Commemorations

The grand spectacle of the Fleet Review and Trafalgar re-enactment was followed by three further large-scale public events. In September the return

---

[24] See, for example, letters page of the Daily Telegraph, 28 June 2005.
[25] Interviews conducted 28 June 2005. (These can be made available as e-files.)
[26] E-mail to the author, 5 July 2005.
[27] The News, 29 June 2005.

of Nelson's body and funeral procession were recreated in a flotilla down the Thames. A month later the Queen lit the first of a chain of beacons to signal the start of the anniversary weekend which culminated in a service of remembrance at St Paul's and a display in Trafalgar Square. All of these events were well supported by the public. As with the Fleet Review, this required large-scale funding and cooperation from many agencies. The government and the machinery of the state were intimately involved, most clearly through the Ministry of Defence. But the events were also supported by other agencies such as the national promoter of tourism, Visit Britain, and the cooperation of the Church of England was vital for the commemoration service at St Paul's Cathedral. Other, smaller, bodies often acted as vital intermediaries and coordinators, such as the 1805 Club organizing the Thames Flotilla, which needed significant help from civil authorities in order to stage the grand spectacle. These events can therefore be judged as 'official' commemorations. Thousands turned out to witness the September flotilla and the October ceremonies, and BBC Two gained a television audience of two million for its highlights programme on Sunday 23 October.[28] In addition, British universities in conjunction with the National Maritime Museum and Royal Naval Museum held two full-scale conferences to explore the battle and its longer-term impacts. A major exhibition on 'Nelson & Napoléon' was mounted at the National Maritime Museum, which sought to put Trafalgar into its full context, exploring issues such as the fad for Egyptian antiquity that was encouraged by the Anglo-French struggles in the shadows of the Pyramids. Finally, a search of Amazon's catalogue revealed that forty-three books on Nelson and Trafalgar were published or reissued in 2005, and the two leading popular history magazines, *History Today* and *BBC History*, produced special editions.[29] Nelson and Trafalgar were therefore celebrated and put before the public in a variety of ways, but as already noted, the actual impact of all this activity is extremely difficult to gauge.

Turning to the media first, it is noticeable that national newspaper coverage of the events took up less space after the June commemorations. Generally, the events were noted and reported succinctly and supportively, but were debated with far less passion than the Fleet Review and battle re-enactment. The only real area of debate continued to be that of the BBC's supposed indifference to, and misunderstanding of, the nature and spirit of the events. A *Daily Telegraph* editorial bemoaned the BBC's coverage of the October events:

---

[28] *Daily Telegraph*, 17 September, 24 October 2005; *The Guardian*, 24 October 2005.
[29] Amazon online catalogue accessed on 5 December 2005, using key word search terms 'Nelson' and 'Trafalgar'; *BBC History*, June 2005; *History Today*, July 2005.

> This weekend, more than 6,000 events will be taking place throughout the British Isles to mark the 200th anniversary of the Battle of Trafalgar. In some of its reports of the bicentenary, the gloomy old BBC has been at pains to suggest that these ceremonies are not a celebration, but a 'commemoration'.
>
> But what nonsense. It is true that hundreds of men and boys were killed in the battle. But it happened so long ago that there is nobody left to suffer grief for the dead, in the way that so many still mourn for the dead of more recent wars. Two hundred years on, the only proper reaction to Nelson's victory is to cheer.
>
> This was the battle that kept the flame of freedom burning in Europe and established our maritime nation as a world power. It laid the foundations for our empire, for our multicultural society and eventually for the good old BBC. Come along, Auntie. Lighten up, be proud to be British—and rejoice![30]

The BBC was in fact being criticized for the organizers' attitudes to the year. As noted, from the very inception of planning, the 2005 events were designed to reveal international cooperation and solidarity in acts of commemoration, not celebration. In accepting the official version of the year, the BBC was misrepresented as a bastion of politically correct attitudes that sought to overturn the supposed true spirit of the events.

Reacting to earlier criticism, the BBC certainly appeared to give a higher priority to the October commemorative events. The Sunday evening digest of the day's London ceremonies allowed viewers to witness highlights plus short documentary inserts which explored Nelson and Trafalgar and provided a brief overview of the events held across the country during 2005. By contrast, relatively few full-scale documentaries or dramas were broadcast by the television companies. Michael Portillo fronted the BBC's sole major documentary contribution, while Channel 4 produced a 'drama-documentary', *Trafalgar Battle Surgeon*, which recreated the battle from the viewpoint of William Beatty, surgeon to HMS *Victory*. The bloodiness of the battle was stressed, along with the intense heroism displayed by the crews of Nelson's fleet. Compared with the attention devoted to the sixtieth anniversary of victory in the Second World War, however, this was not a major effort.

Indeed, the June celebrations were rapidly eclipsed by three events. First, the long-planned sixtieth anniversary commemorations deflected attention to the crucial event in modern British culture, the Second World War.[31] Second, the G8 summit and Live 8 events were given large-scale coverage in the press, with the BBC providing full, live coverage of the Live 8 concert in

---

[30] *Daily Telegraph*, 22 October 2005.
[31] For the impact of the Second World War on contemporary British culture, see Mark Connelly, *We Can Take It! Britain and the Memory of the Second World War* (London, 2003).

Hyde Park. Third, and intimately connected with these points, the terrorist bombings on 7 July served to increase the profile of the sixtieth anniversary commemorations as they reinforced the historicized British lessons of the Second World War: defiance in the face of terror and dedication to the values of democracy and toleration.

Given the sobering impact of the bombings, and the outpourings of national pride and remembrance that formed a central part of the sixtieth anniversary celebrations, the Trafalgar commemorations faced a difficult job in trying to regain public interest when they returned in September. Significantly, public reaction to the events continued to show a marked variance from the values set down by the organizers, and it is equally difficult to trace any great increase in knowledge of Nelson, Trafalgar, and the sea. In wishing to stress international cooperation and friendship, the organizers were at odds with wider public perceptions. Confusion was then created by the events themselves, with their veneer of internationalism and reconciliation, which sat strangely with the overt celebrations of the Royal Navy and British maritime history. For example, the commemorations of Sunday 23 October were described as a moment when all those who participated and fell in the battle would be remembered, and that spirit was an important theme in the Bishop of London's address at the St Paul's service. Such an approach contrasted strongly with the full-blooded celebration of the Royal Navy that followed in Trafalgar Square, culminating in an exciting recreation of a Royal Marines operation to round up drug-traffickers. This second element was probably far more in tune with public attitudes, and may have helped reinforce the popularly desired history lessons. Examination of locally organized regional events certainly reveals a much stronger patriotic theme.

A Regional Study

East Anglia, the region of Nelson's birth, provides a good example. The *East Anglian Daily Times* issued a commemorative special edition in honour of 'The Greatest East Anglian' and was unstinting in its praise of Wellington's and Nelson's victories, stating that 'we still salute both men's brilliant leadership in war.'[32] On Trafalgar Day, East Anglia threw itself into an unalloyed celebration of local and national identity. At Southwold the former mayor and current councillor commenced the celebrations by playing the National Anthem on his trumpet. In Ipswich local primary schools spent

[32] *East Anglian Daily Times*, 22 October 2005.

all week turning their classrooms into recreations of Nelson's fleet, while at Mersea Island School in Essex a rowing boat was converted into HMS *Victory* and the children dressed up as sailors. Children at White Notley Primary School made special banners which they paraded through the streets in their home-made naval costumes, built a model of HMS *Victory*, and sent signals by flag semaphore. Colchester held a storytelling event, and a special parade and service of remembrance to celebrate local men who were involved in the battle, while traders in Chelmsford market decorated their stalls with Union flags, and at Braintree the White Ensign flew from the town hall. 'We are proud to be marking the Battle of Trafalgar and that we are able to show this by flying the White Ensign', said council leader, Graham Butland.[33] The photographs in the *East Anglian Daily Times*, *Essex Times*, and *Essex Chronicle* reveal a rich profusion of Union flags, crosses of St George, and White Ensigns, as well as a few pirates![34] Moving to the extreme west of Britain, the organizers of Northern Ireland's events saw it as a chance to stress the links between its local identity and the wider one of the United Kingdom, culminating in the presentation of the freedom of the Borough of North Down to the crew of HMS *Bangor*.[35] Such displays of local and national patriotism entwined show that the official tone of reconciliation was either rejected or ignored in regional celebrations. Further, it also reveals a greater element of democracy. Although local events were clearly the result of organization and cooperation with various civil authorities, there was, clearly, far more latitude for the display of opinions and attitudes at variance from the ONCC's overall tone. At the same time, it proves the ONCC's belief that popular re-engagement with Nelson could be inspired even if it followed a very different agenda.

Reactions

These events also reveal a genuine desire to provide children with a historical education no matter how much professionals might debate its worth and significance. As noted, popular ignorance of 1805 was an issue of widespread concern at the start of the year, and both the concern and

[33] *Essex County Standard*, 21 October 2005; *Essex Chronicle*, 27 October 2005; *Essex Times*, 26 October 2005.

[34] *East Anglian Daily Times*, 22 October 2005; *Essex Chronicle*, 27 October 2005; *Essex Times*, 26 October 2005.

[35] Information supplied by Lieutenant-Commander Peter Archdale, 10 September 2005. Bangor is the county town of Down.

the ignorance were in evidence throughout the commemorations. David Derbyshire, the *Daily Telegraph's* reporter on the beachfront for the Fleet Review, remarked on the extreme vagueness of many, especially among the young. One young woman with A-level history stated that Trafalgar played no part in her studies; a man of eighteen with GCSE History was equally lost, believing the battle took place in 1743 after a French landing. Of three female friends in their mid-thirties, only one was fully aware of the significance of the day and had brought her five-year-old son along in order to help his education. Those over forty showed a good deal more knowledge, including eighty-four-year-old Wilbert Anderson, who originated in Jamaica. Now resident in Birmingham, he had come down with his son and daughter-in-law, and stated: 'We are patriotic . . . and people from the Caribbean have always seen themselves as British.'[36] My own interviews revealed a similar pattern. Those of an age to have small children (generally those aged between thirty and forty) revealed a deep emotional connection with the navy and British history unsupported by any real knowledge, but felt equally strongly that their children should be given a thorough education in British national history and heroes.[37]

The need to foreground British history in education remained a continual theme throughout the commemorations. Richard Chartres, the Bishop of London, used his address at the St Paul's service to condemn the imbalanced nature of the National Curriculum's approach to History. Referring to his daughter's studies in History, he remarked on its lack of chronological integrity and obsession with contemporary matters, which prized knowledge of subjects like the Vietnam War and Twiggy and instilled no sense of context or true perspective. He stated: 'There has never been a generation better informed about "now" with so little sense of how we came to be here', and added, 'Every child in this country ought to have the opportunity of meeting Lord Nelson and considering his legacy.'[38] The same day School Inspectors were reported as advocating the compulsory teaching of History up to the age of at least sixteen. The Ofsted Report noted: 'Pupils often do not know about key historical events, people and ideas and there is often unjustified repetition of topics', and referred to fears 'about our national identity' created by confused History curricula.[39] The *Daily Telegraph's* Ferdinand Mount returned to these points, and added: 'It is not simply a matter of education in patriotism, though that reason cannot be sneered at. Even those who do not care for the sound of gunfire need to

[36] *Daily Telegraph*, 29 June 2005.
[37] I did not ask people to provide their age; the figures given above are my estimates.
[38] *Daily Telegraph*, 24 October 2005.
[39] Ibid., 23 October 2005.

know all about Nelson, because, as well as being the bravest and most brilliant of leaders, he was also the most controversial.' He then suggested that
the government should set a new educational target of teaching all British
schoolchildren to spell out 'England Expects Every Man Will Do His Duty'
in flags within two years.[40] Commemorating Trafalgar, Nelson, and the
Royal Navy, therefore, served to spark a debate about British educational
practice and its vital significance in creating citizens firmly grounded in a
common culture and history. Those critical of current practices were
unmoved by any questioning of a nationalistic element, and indeed saw this
as the missing vital ingredient.

A month after the Fleet Review I interviewed fourteen Year 9 boys at the
Simon Langton Boys' Grammar School, Canterbury. Despite the coverage of
the events, very few of the boys were aware of the celebrations, and only one
felt any real connection with the sea, largely because his family owned a boat
and took part in water sports. Nelson was confused with Napoleon, none
knew the name of Nelson's flagship, only seven had heard of the Battle of
Trafalgar, and only one had been to the National Maritime Museum.[41]
Significantly, very few of these boys connected the sea with their own travel
experiences. We now live in the 'Easyjet generation'. With the advent of
cheap air travel and ever greater competition in the package holiday market,
families take their holidays abroad, and their experience of the sea and boats
is now usually the Mediterranean and pedalos rather than Scarborough and
a boat trip around the bay. In terms of consumer culture, ferries have become
more and more a cross between aircraft and shopping malls. Deck spaces have
disappeared and promenade spaces are now often enclosed, serving to shield
passengers from the sea and elements. There is little encouragement to con-
template the sea and passengers are instead distracted by shopping, eating, and
audio-visual displays of films, music videos, and video games. However, the
success of the recent BBC documentary series, *Coast* (2005), may be the first
revelation of a slowly flowering renaissance of knowledge and interest.

During 2005 academic debate of the bicentenary revealed the diversity
of study on Nelson and the battle.[42] The conferences and National
Maritime Museum exhibition were sophisticated and wide-ranging explor-
ations of the man, the society in which he lived, and the legacies of his great
victory. Yet it is extremely doubtful whether this had any meaningful
impact on wider public perceptions and the public debate. The popular histories of Trafalgar which poured out, and were epitomized by Tim Clayton

---

[40] *Daily Telegraph*, 28 October 2005.
[41] Interviews conducted on 18 July 2005. (These can be made available as e-files.)
[42] For a useful overview of the new, and reprinted, literature see John Brewer, 'The return
of the imperial hero', *New York Review of Books*, 3 November 2005.

and Phil Craig's highly readable *Trafalgar: The Men, the Battle, the Storm*, provided colour, action, adventure, and heroes in abundance. (Significantly, the authors had provided a blueprint for themselves in their account of Britain's twentieth-century equivalent, the year 1940, in *Finest Hour*.) Academic history was at marked variance with popular perceptions. Adam Nicolson's *Seize the Fire: Heroism, Duty and the Battle of Trafalgar* applied a cultural history template to the battle. He sought to understand the battle in terms of the *mentalité* of its protagonists, exploring the way psyches were shaped and the imperatives these forces brought to individual actions. Nelson emerges from such works as an extremely complex character. He was a man of improvisation *and* intense planning; a man capable of ignoring orders and yet demanding action from subordinates on the tiniest details. These polarities were explored in David Cannadine's edited collection of essays, *Admiral Lord Nelson: Context and Legacy*. Kate Williams's essay, 'Nelson and women', reveals the tensions between Nelson as the apogee of stoical masculinity, and the man of great feeling unafraid to break cultural norms by expressing it in writing and oratory. The essays by Colin White and Holger Hoock show how carefully Nelson created his own image, and then how others used him for other purposes. Bringing the full rigour of academic scrutiny to the Battle of Trafalgar and its legacy inspired work of the highest quality, but it did not meet the demand for emotional, public history. Popular perceptions of Nelson and Trafalgar were either extremely hazy, due to a lack of hard knowledge, and do not appear to have changed much as a result of the events, or determined to ensure that a highly traditional, Whiggish interpretation should succeed unfettered by any negative debate about the glory of his achievements. The section of the public that became involved with the commemorations did so on an emotional level and demanded that historians give them an unambiguous celebration of British achievement, but the academy was not quite happy with that role. Figures such as Colin White attempted to walk the tightrope. His passion for Nelson and the Navy was translated into a host of talks, articles, and a new edition of Nelson's letters. In his work, and indeed mission, he valiantly attempted to straddle the divide between providing the public with a hero and maintaining a sense of balance and detachment. His dilemma mirrored that which exists more generally between academic and public history. So-called 'informed opinion' was often convinced that the modern public demanded a more nuanced Nelson, the fully rounded man of faults as well as great attributes. And yet many of the comments made about the commemorations emphasized the failure to stress the greatness of the achievement and the man, and that a reluctance to press the patriotic case had left a degree of unwanted ambiguity in the air. The arousal of such passions might be seen as a result of the commemorations; at least one aim of the commemorations committee was therefore achieved: Nelson and his legacy are again being debated in Britain. However, will the debate and interest last, and have knowledge and awareness really increased? It is hard to escape a negative conclusion. Only by direct state intervention in the National Curriculum can the role of the navy, Nelson, and the sea be more fully instilled in British life.

In conclusion, the commemorations aroused debate about Nelson, and attracted and touched the lives of thousands of people, but it is doubtful whether they made many new converts to the ONCC's mission. Where interest was aroused among new constituents, particularly among schools that took part in the commemorative events with enthusiasm such as those in the East Anglian and Portsmouth areas, momentum can be maintained only by positive governmental action. For all the tremendous efforts made to commemorate the anniversary year, and all the many well-supported events, there is very little reason why Sellar and Yeatman's version should not remain the orthodoxy unless there is a major change to the National Curriculum and a sustained alteration in the way the sea is presented and experienced in everyday British life. If this task is to be achieved, the academy will have to find a way of balancing the disciplines of History against the public demand for History to act as a repository of national triumphs and tragedies, each with a clear balance sheet and set of moral–spiritual lessons.

6.

The National Maritime Museum's 2005 Exhibition, 'Nelson & Napoléon': Intention and Reception

MARGARETTE LINCOLN AND MARTIN DAUNTON

Commemorating

Commemorating anniversaries is a staple of museum exhibitions, television programmes, and press articles. The changing manner of memorializing key moments in national history gives historians access to cultural meanings and interpretations of national identity—and no event offers a greater insight than the Battle of Trafalgar, with its popular hero Horatio, Lord Nelson. Trafalgar Square and Nelson's Column mean that the battle and the admiral remain more central to British life than any other figure from the Napoleonic wars—even Wellington, and certainly William Pitt the Younger. But the centrality of Nelson in national memory posed particular issues at the bicentenary of his death. In 1905, the centenary of the battle and Nelson's death coincided with the accelerating naval race with Germany and the construction of the *Dreadnought*. The story was not uncomplicated, for many free-trading Liberals feared militarism and excessive spending—and the Entente Cordiale of 1904 with France constrained too much celebration of defeat of the old enemy. The bicentenary in 2005 posed different problems.

This essay will focus on the National Maritime Museum's 2005 exhibition, 'Nelson & Napoléon'. Though large, it was one event of many in the UK-wide, SeaBritain 2005 programme, which was initiated by the Museum to commemorate Trafalgar but also to celebrate Britain's maritime heritage more widely. For the past thirty years, the National Maritime Museum has harnessed anniversaries for big exhibitions to help attract audiences, and it initiated the Official Nelson Celebration (later Commemoration) Committee (ONCC) essentially for this reason in 1995. The timing was dictated by its gallery refurbishment programme that scheduled a redesigned Nelson Gallery in that year. As no convenient Nelsonic anniversary fell then, the vehicle of 'the Nelson Decade' was invented when the exhibition was launched, and the formation of the ONCC announced to coincide with this exhibition. The intention had long been to cooperate with other museums and societies, since the Nelson and Trafalgar assets were dispersed: Greenwich had the collections, but Portsmouth had the *Victory* and the Royal Naval Museum, and significant collections were in smaller institutions, as well as in private hands. It also made very good sense for the Nelson Society and the 1805 Club to join the ONCC deliberations, not least because there was some distance between the two societies at that time. And it was important to get the Royal Navy enthused: it was not until very close to the event that it committed itself to any preparations for marking the bicentenary of Trafalgar. From the start, there were good business and political reasons for the zeal for Nelson, and when Roy Clare became Director of the National Maritime Museum in 2000, this cooperative structure was extended to a nationwide coordination effort through SeaBritain 2005. This framework resulted in unprecedented partnerships across the country that are likely to be sustained to help with future initiatives.

Interpretations

Yet at one meeting of the trustees of the National Maritime Museum, the issue of whether the battle and Nelson should be commemorated in any special way at all was seriously considered. Was Nelson still sufficiently well known, or was he an iconic figure only for a certain segment of the population? Would he appeal to women visitors? How would he appeal to ethnic minorities, given that Nelson either played no role in their own histories, or appeared as a symbol of imperial exploitation and support for slavery? Was the answer to stress the role of women in the life of the British navy, and to point to the multicultural nature of the fleet? Or was it to address in an explicit way the role of the British navy in extending the Empire, making links with the defence of Caribbean sugar plantations and expansion in India? Should Nelson be portrayed less as a protector of British liberties from Napoleonic ambitions and more as a defender of slavery? Or should the aim be to show how the two might be reconciled in the minds of many at the time, and attacked as incompatible by others? How could the picture of Nelson as a great popular hero, the name of a thousand public houses, be reconciled with his participation in a British state seen by many radicals at the time (and since) as repressive and a threat to civil liberties? And how could the events of Trafalgar be presented without incurring the dangers of nationalistic celebrations of defeat of the French?

The decision to mark the bicentenary of Trafalgar and the death of Nelson was surely correct, but the question of how to navigate these treacherous waters was not easily resolved. The obvious answer was to place the battle and the life of Nelson in a wider context of international strategy. Why did Trafalgar matter? How did it fit into the much longer conflict between Britain and France over the previous century, and their tussle for domination? One way of undertaking this task would have been to place Nelson in a longer line of heroic admirals and how they were viewed at the time—men such as Rodney or Howe. Dashing admirals might be compared with gallant generals such as Wolfe and Wellington, and the role of the navy and army in British politics, society, culture, and economy teased out. What part did they play in Parliament, how significant were the dockyards and barracks in the economy, how did the state raise money to finance massive spending on war, how were the exploits of the army and navy celebrated and commemorated, and who were the rank-and-file? Another way of undertaking the task would be to focus in depth on the events of the French Revolutionary and Napoleonic wars, analysing the battles of Trafalgar and Waterloo, and the careers and personalities of Nelson and Wellington. Such an approach would allow the place of Ireland and India, and of warfare on land in Europe and the Empire, to be integrated with exploits on the sea, to produce a sense of the worldwide strategy pursued by Britain. Connections could also be made with the internal affairs of different countries in Europe—with events in Spain during the Peninsular campaign, in Prussia, and the drama at Waterloo, and domestically within Britain in the form of popular unrest, financial pressures, and industrial development.

In fact, the approach adopted was a third way—comparing Nelson with Napoleon in order to use the anniversary and the exhibition to set Nelson's achievements in a wider, European context. The attractions were obvious. A double and equal billing of an Englishman and a Frenchman dealt with the issue of nationalism—though with the potential difficulties of criticism precisely on the ground that a great British hero was devalued by comparison with a continental tyrant. The dual focus also offered a way of dealing with the wider strategic issues of the war between Britain and France, and the internal dynamics of the two societies, through an accessible biographical approach. And the two men allowed an exploration of how highly significant and iconic lives were memorialized and contested after their deaths. Equally, there were drawbacks. Nelson died in battle in 1805; Napoleon's career continued. The lack of chronological symmetry was compounded by differences in their roles: Nelson was a sailor and little more; Napoleon was a general and much more besides. And how easy would it be to bring out elements of the wider picture which might have been more possible through one of the other two approaches?

The National Maritime Museum maintains a permanent Nelson gallery at Greenwich, because so many visitors come specifically to see Nelson's uniform that it is always on display. The latest reworking of that gallery, completed in 1995, had already focused on Nelson's career and explored the nature of his heroic status—although the result was so subtle that few noticed any hint of questioning. For the 2005 anniversary, the Museum was determined to move away from an examination of Nelson's character and career, and because so much of its Nelsonia was on permanent display anyway, it seemed that the new exhibition would need something special to make visitors think an additional trip to Greenwich worthwhile. Since no other museum has a comparable Nelson collection, curators had a comparatively free hand and the choice of concept was not constrained by other planned exhibitions about Trafalgar. The Museum aimed to include a significant element of cultural history in its exhibition in order to show the broad reach of maritime history and to reinforce the message that it is not narrowly interested in naval history alone. In all its work the Museum aims to help bring naval affairs back into the history of Britain and to demonstrate that if you do not understand maritime history, you can never fully understand Britain. This has been a conscious strategy for the past decade. In this sense the anniversary offered a welcome opportunity for the Museum to address under-represented aspects of historical education and enhance public debate.

The Museum had hoped that by coupling Nelson with Napoleon, it would excite and intrigue audiences and help to avoid a resolutely British perspective. Curators aimed for a better understanding of the significance of Nelson's victories but never simply to explore Anglo-French relations, as some critics implied. Labels and wall panels were printed in English and French, with no variation in the literal meaning and no attempt to pander to national prejudice. The Museum also included in the exhibition aspects of social history: the lives of ordinary seamen and the women left at home. This was an occasion to bring together many objects in one place and to give an insight into these complex years of warfare. The practical constraints of any exhibition mean that subtleties and qualifications sometimes have to be sacrificed to brevity. For example, the Spanish perspective, though important, had to be largely omitted for reasons of space. Exhibition curators also had to find means to overcome a real chronological difficulty in order to achieve a coherent and satisfying conclusion: Nelson died prematurely in 1805 while Napoleon went on to win great victories on land before defeat at Waterloo, death in exile on St Helena in 1821, and the return of his remains to France in 1840.

The Museum has achieved a well-deserved reputation for being able to mount exhibitions on complex historical issues with tact, intelligence, and style. The 'Nelson & Napoléon' exhibition was a thought-provoking and well-crafted show that drew upon both internal and external expertise, taking advantage of the Museum's strong links with academia. There was a series of advisory meetings with specialists in maritime history at concept stage. Nicholas Rodger also acted as Historical Consultant, Holger Hoock as Research Curator, and Colin White came to Greenwich on a four-year secondment from the Royal Naval Museum, Portsmouth, as Director, Trafalgar 200. In many ways, the exhibition's broad sweep mirrored the reshaping of approaches to maritime topics adopted by historians. Also, in order to address the needs of specific audiences and deal with complex issues in more depth, as usual the Museum scheduled a range of activities around its major exhibition. There was a scholarly catalogue containing introductory essays that treated its themes from a range of perspectives, a joint international conference with the Institute of Historical Research that was booked to capacity, and focused learning programmes for all ages.

No solution is ideal, and any approach is a compromise between the complexities of the historical interpretation, the availability of material objects, and political calculations of current sensitivities. Many visitors might wish to pay homage to Nelson as a great naval hero and nationalistic figurehead—but the curators might wish to make them think about the wider European strategy within which he operated, the tedium of the blockade, and the nature of the navy. The curators might be accused of political correctness and of subverting national identity by the right; and of failing to emphasize the exploitation of workers at home and the threats to civil liberties by the left. Inevitably, any major exhibition is limited by space, the availability of material objects, and the constraints of captions—and informed by current concerns and events, a factor which intruded all too obviously into the timing of the exhibition at a time of British involvement in another war, and a terrorist attack in London.

Reception

On one level, the decision was clearly correct, for the 'Nelson & Napoléon' exhibition at the National Maritime Museum was enormously successful: 91,000 people came to see it during a difficult period for tourism in London, and an independent survey by MORI was overwhelmingly positive, with 96 per cent of visitors rating the exhibition highly and 94 per cent saying that they would recommend it to others. An unprecedented range of material was put on display, some of which had never before been seen in

Britain or in public. Yet the opening of the exhibition on 7 July 2005 coincided with the terrorist bombings in London. The evening reception had to be cancelled, but, more important, all scheduled television coverage of the exhibition was wiped out by exclusive media focus on the terrorist atrocities. Television has pre-eminence in formulating public opinion; a particular loss was the slot on the chat show *Newsnight Review*, which would have permitted intelligent discussion of the exhibition from different perspectives. The Museum therefore had to rely more heavily on press coverage of the exhibition to encourage people, now far more reluctant to travel across London, to visit the show. The marketing campaign was refocused to give greater emphasis on the local press and on locations extending towards the M25 that would allow potential visitors travelling to Greenwich to avoid central London.

The exhibition seemed on course to be intelligently reviewed and enjoyed by a receptive audience. A preview in the *Eastern Daily Press*, published on its first day, accurately noted that the new show offered a perspective of the age in which both men lived and fought as well as insights into their personal lives and the impact of the French wars on Britain, remarking that it placed the implications and brutal reality of war alongside the intimacy of certain objects, such as Nelson's last letter to his daughter Horatia.[1] The coincidence of the bombings with the opening allowed some perceptive and intelligent reviewers to assimilate the exhibition's construction of the past into contemporary politics. Joan Bakewell in *The Guardian* included the exhibition in a wide-ranging 'think-piece' on the bombings, its effect on concepts of 'Britishness' and on decisions about asylum-seekers, arguing that we need to preserve the cool, analytical gaze of history if we are to make the right decisions about asylum. She noted that there was nothing wrong in setting Nelson alongside Napoleon: 'If we perceive these events as far enough in the past, we view them as history. The blood has cooled. Distance mutes the outrage at human aggression and brutality.' The piece underlines the relevance of the historical process of museum exhibitions, and their social importance in demonstrating the value of rigorous thought, regardless of immediate subject. It also helps to throw light on the role of historical anniversaries in historical education and public history.[2] Unfortunately, the main response to the horror of the London suicide bombs was less perceptive. The immediate effect was to blot out much of the initial press coverage in the national newspapers, and later reviews tended to focus safely on Nelson the man and hero, and even to view the

---

[1] *Eastern Daily Press*, 7 July 2005, 31.
[2] *The Guardian*, G2 section, 29 July 2005, 12.

juxtaposition of the two men as overly contrived or as demonstrating unnecessary political correctness.

It is difficult to know how much notice visitors take of reviews. In a sense all press coverage is worth having, but while visitors to the exhibition may have been enlightened, its role in the construction of the past for those who only glanced at newspaper reviews is more problematic. Arts reviewers for the press always seem to have difficulty commenting on mixed-media exhibitions that offer strong narratives. One of the earliest reviews, a superficial piece by Rhoda Koenig of *The Independent*, failed to notice that the Museum had explicitly stated that it did not intend to equate the two men. She accused the Museum of being intrinsically unfair to Napoleon because the exhibition did not dwell on his domestic policy and focused on a summary detail: 'the Code Napoleon, for instance, is referred to only in passing, with no explanation, on a label near the exit.'[3] It might equally be pointed out that the exhibition said little about British domestic politics—whether on the achievements of Pitt in funding the war, or on the pressures of warfare on the economy. The *Independent on Sunday* for 24 July questioned the very basis of the exhibition, humorously citing the authors of *1066 and All That*, who had cautioned that 'Napoleon ought never to be confused with Nelson, in spite of their hats being so alike.'[4] The reviewer also assumed that the Museum was simply intent on comparing the two men and crisply noted that the suggestion of equivalence flattered Nelson, 'a brilliant but rather narrow man, whose conversation was said to be limited principally to naval tactics'. Here was an opportunity lost. The two men had more than their height in common: both were anxiously concerned about their public image and Napoleon in particular demonstrated great skill in manipulating and disseminating his. Greater emphasis on this point would have enabled interesting modern parallels to be considered. Instead, the newspaper took the exhibition's larger theme to be Anglo-French relations and a parallel was drawn between the envy and wariness with which Britain regarded France in the early nineteenth century and the emotion of the crowd waiting in Trafalgar Square for the 2012 Olympic announcement. Quite gratuitously, the spectre of jingoism that so often accompanies contemporary sporting contests was raised again.

Rachel Campbell-Johnston's review in *The Times* did note that the Museum was attempting to be European rather than narrowly British in its outlook but she also drew specific attention to personal items, commenting that it was when the exhibition 'focuses on the personal that it touches

---

[3] *The Independent*, 13 July 2005, 44.
[4] *Independent on Sunday*, 24 July 2005, 11.

the spectator to the quick'.[5] She concluded that 'this is a show that conjures the atmosphere of a period. The spirits that haunt it send a shiver down the spine'—a phrase that the Museum adopted in its renewed marketing campaign for the exhibition after the London bombings affected visitor numbers. The immediacy of objects—of the bloodstained garments worn by Nelson, or Beethoven's furious erasure of the dedication of the Eroica symphony to Napoleon—allow people to empathize with people in the past in a way that books or even TV programmes cannot. The terrorist attack seemingly encouraged empathy with suffering, and this emphasis on the personal was invariably replicated in later reviews. *The Observer* on 17 July considered that although the exhibition placed the men in their historical context, it was the personal rather the political that stood out and that what emerged was chiefly the personalities of these two diminutive men who had once towered over the fortunes of Europe.[6] In fact, one of the Museum's aims had been to consider how the fortunes of both Nelson and Napoleon had been somehow enabled by the turbulent times in which they lived, although the structure of the gallery, which juxtaposed images of the two men, may have encouraged a more personal comparison.

In general, the national press focused on Nelson's life rather than on the wonderful objects in the exhibition. *The Observer* of 17 July considered that the highlights were two large paintings (*The Death of Nelson* by Arthur William Devis, which depicts Nelson at the point of death wrapped in a shroud-like white sheet and radiating light as if the glory of the next world is already upon him, and *Napoleon as First Consul* by Jean-Auguste-Dominique Ingres, a full-length portrait and one of five sent to towns in northern France to remind citizens of their loyalty to the new regime), but reviewers more commonly picked up on the personal relics preserved from Nelson's wounding and death. 'It is all here: no medieval saint could have asked for more,' commented Adam Nicolson in the *Sunday Telegraph*, 'the French musket ball that killed him . . . the coat he was wearing when he was shot . . . the bloodstained waistcoat . . . his stockings . . . his breeches . . . Nelson's velvet stock . . . his hair and pigtail.'[7] The Museum did emphasize that it had reunited objects for dramatic effect: the two betrothal rings exchanged by Nelson and Emma, Horatia's christening cup and spoon, the fatal musket ball with a fragment of gold braid still attached and Nelson's torn coat. Yet arts reviewers seem more comfortable with great paintings and, as Brian Sewell rightly remarked, the exhibition necessarily contained fewer such items than the Museum's previous blockbuster exhibition,

[5] *The Times*, T2 section, 13 July 2005, 11–12.
[6] *The Observer*, 17 July 2005, 12.
[7] *Sunday Telegraph*, Review section, 17 July 2005, 5.

'Elizabeth'. Also, the paintings which reviewers commonly focused on simply supported the apparent comparison between the two men. Advertising features published in the provincial press (notably in the naval towns of Portsmouth and Plymouth) proved an exception, in that they did not focus on Nelson's life. Instead, they emphasized the range of objects in the exhibition and the fact that it incorporated new research that challenged old myths, but these features were 'puffs' rather than reviews, which did little more than re-present the Museum's own press releases. Given the increasing importance of media representation in the construction of the past, it is a matter for unease that in a world of events competing for media attention important exhibitions are reviewed so scantly. Exhibitions do not generally set out to provide a clear starting point for debate but aim to present the latest scholarship and to change worn-out perceptions. All the same, the public deserves better and more thoughtful press discussion of the serious issues raised in museum displays.

Most of the attendant events in 2005, whether official, commercial, or popular, celebrated Nelson and may have helped to predispose audiences to take a similar personal perspective on the exhibition at Greenwich. Programmed activities provided a boost for tourism, a range of publishing opportunities for both academic and popular books on maritime history, and a variety of television programmes from BBC Two's *Coast*, unjustifiably neglected, to Channel 4's *Rum, Sodomy and the Lash* purporting to tell viewers what it was really like for the ordinary men—and women—in Nelson's navy. All contributed to our collective construction of the past and underlined the point that maritime heritage helps to define our sense of identity as 'an island nation'. The major auction houses all held well-publicized sales of Nelson material in 2005, which may also have helped to keep the man and hero in the public eye. The commemorative events of that year naturally helped to inflate auction house prices for Nelsonic items and many were put on the market. Nelson's undershirt, for example, was predicted to sell for as much as half a million pounds, having been hyped as possibly worn by the hero at Trafalgar. Though interesting as a rare survival of contemporary underwear, which was usually re-purposed in an age more attuned to recycling, no one credited that Nelson had actually been wearing the garment when fatally shot: there were no bloodstains, the hole was on the wrong side and seemed more likely to have been made by moths. Yet the media enthusiastically picked up on these items and successive, high-profile auctions helped to focus attention on the hero, his life and personality in a more adulatory way than was the intention in the Museum's exhibition.

The Museum, in grounding its exhibition in social and cultural history, deliberately tried to feminize the maritime anniversary by including objects belonging to ordinary naval women, in addition to referencing both Emma and Josephine, who were clearly germane to the narrative. *The Lady* magazine duly picked up on this, beginning its lively review of the Nelson exhibition with, 'His affair with a flame-haired ex-artist's model who had married into the aristocracy scandalised genteel society', and later focusing on the more 'poignant' objects.[8] Yet this merely perpetuated Emma's already existent notoriety and was by no means enough to counteract the focus of the majority of newspapers on elements calculated to appeal more to a male constituency who were indeed the main audience. The Museum had also understood that it would need to work hard to extend the appeal of the exhibition to young people. The interactive exhibit, woefully misunderstood by the reviewer in *The Lady* as 'an audio-visual display projected on to a vast naval tracking chart that is suspended from the ceiling', employed the latest infra-red technology in an effort to attract enthusiastic younger visitors. It certainly conveyed the fact that at Trafalgar all the ships were independently moving as they tried to engage each other and that the confusion of battle must have been great. All in vain; the prime audience for the exhibition remained predominantly elderly and male.

Educational programmes linked to the exhibition certainly compensated for this. The Museum's special courses for sixth-form business studies students, which examined Nelson's leadership qualities and linked transferable skills to historical content, proved extremely popular. The Museum had produced a similar programme and education pack on Elizabeth I for its 'Elizabeth' exhibition in 2003, and the use of popular historical figures to teach leadership skills constitutes a new means of commemorating and memorializing as students are asked to probe events, issues, and change over time. Purists might object that history is being misused in an anachronistic way, taking past behaviour out of context; pragmatists might accept that students and sponsors are being made to think about historical material they might otherwise ignore. The accompanying publication was shortlisted for an Arts and Business Award. The Museum's Nelson-related projects for gifted and talented secondary school students, which focused on the development of techniques for historical enquiry and on presentation skills, were equally successful. In all, over 4,000 visited the exhibition in booked school groups, and in these ways the exhibition did much to educate young people as well as confirm others in their respect for Nelson's achievements. The Museum also put its Nelson collection online, enabling it to extend its reach to other audiences. Over the summer months the promotion of the Nelson content led to a big jump in visitor numbers to the

[8] *The Lady*, 5–11 July 2005, 34–5.

Museum's website. A blockbuster exhibition like 'Nelson & Napoléon' always stimulates new research and acts as a focus for learning programmes at different levels.

Correspondents writing for religious newspapers provided some interesting takes on the show. Under the headline 'Nautical but nice', Joy Sable of the *Jewish Chronicle* gave a contextual review of the exhibition, filling in the historical background for readers seemingly without much of a clue: 'At that time, Britain was at war with France and Spain, and life as a sailor was a dangerous business.' However, she too focused on Nelson the man rather than on the quality of the objects in the exhibition.[9] Graham Gendall Norton in the *Church of England Newspaper* began his review by noting that the opening of the exhibition had coincided with the London bomb attacks; his criticism of the exhibition as politically correct therefore made it seem an example of risky liberalism. Commenting on the labels in French and English, he added, 'and why not, as francophone visitors will want to visit this curious contrived conjunction'. He emphasized the point that Nelson was a parson's son, noted that the exhibition featured Nelson's final prayer and quoted it at length, 'May the Great God, whom I worship, grant to my country and for the benefit of Europe in general a great and glorious victory . . .'. Missing the point that Nelson at least was thinking in a European context, he then noted that the first comma 'smacks to me as much of 18th-century deism as of Christianity'. His point is an interesting one, and more could have been made of the intellectual and religious dimension of the French and British, of the differences and similarities of the enlightenment in the two countries. The 'natural' theology of Anglicanism was just as much at ease with scientific progress as French enlightenment thinkers. Gendall Norton went on to complain that Nelson had no qualms about hanging mutineers on a Sunday and was an open adulterer—Lady Hamilton was not, he suspected, Nelson's only mistress, and he alluded to 'other, more casual liaisons'. Perhaps there could have been more development of the theme of masculinity and moral behaviour—of the sexual licence tolerated by so many, and opposed by moral reformers. Gendall Norton complained that the Museum had not been sufficiently critical of Nelson, that curators had glossed over his vanity, his active assistance 'in the judicial murder of revolutionaries in Naples, who surrendered in the expectation of clemency, inappropriately involving HM ships in the internal affairs of another country', and his strong support for the slave trade.[10] He speculated in a counter-factual way that had Nelson the hero lived, been rewarded with a dukedom, and spoken in the House

[9] *Jewish Chronicle*, 22 July 2005, 37.
[10] *Church of England Newspaper*, 29 July 2005, 21.

of Lords, it would have been far harder to pass the bill abolishing the British slave trade in 1807. He does have a point, and his comments bring out the highly contested nature of historical reputations both at the time and since. A comparison with Wellington would elucidate this very clearly: the great general survived to become the force of reaction and oppression. Gendall Norton also disapproved of the paintings representing Nelson's apotheosis. Seemingly oblivious to nineteenth-century artistic conventions, he commented finally, 'am I the only one to sense something sacrilegious in the final paintings?' Devis's deliberate use of the iconography of the deposition of Christ was in fact one of the most interesting aspects of the show for an art historian. Indeed, a criticism of the show might be that more was not made of contemporary artistic conventions.

Adam Nicolson, perhaps the only reviewer to engage deeply with the objects in the exhibition, pondered on the strangeness of the historical objects on display, which at once invited intimacy and yet gave insights into a culture which remained remote and incomprehensible. He noted Beatty's delicate instrument case — 'filled with the spirit of enlightenment' but used in a place of horror, and marvelled at the central strangeness of war: the meticulous tailoring drenched in blood, the rationalist instruments designed to treat brutal wounds. He admitted that 'this sense of unreality is not of course the intention of the organisers. The exhibition aims not to demonstrate the searing hole which battle cuts in cultural life, but its opposite', namely to set the war in its cultural context. Yet his comments perpetuate a view of the enlightenment as a realm of precision and order that has often been challenged and which the exhibition itself put to the test. However, Nicolson did address the ideological confrontation between France and Britain and their conflicting notions of liberty, offering a fascinating comparison of the two nations' ideological imagery. French propagandist material seemed to him so much smarter than the British — examples of 'a dazzling and powerful chic that leaves the British trailing'. He wondered if the real question answered by the exhibition is 'why we won' — that the freewheeling, entrepreneurial Britons succeeded more than French chic and its stylish culture. Sadly, Nicolson's discussion, which began with an interesting consideration of different notions of liberty, ultimately did little more than replicate national stereotypes.

Yet nothing so sophisticated materialized in the French press. There were notices in magazines aimed at tourists that described the highlights of the exhibition, but no lengthy reviews. Exhibition curators were interviewed on French television by presenters who tried to excite controversy around national agendas and focused on provocative questions of national identity. While curators stressed that the exhibition aimed to be balanced and that there had been bravery on both sides at Trafalgar, French interviewers insinuated that perhaps the exhibition originated in a desire to crow over French defeat. *France Magazine* was determined to be more diplomatic—citing evidence in the exhibition to show that at least Napoleon swiftly mastered English, even if he did not manage to overrun the country. It also quoted a BBC interview of the Fondation Napoléon's historian to the effect that Napoleon 'was not necessarily anti-English. He had to fight because [Britain] was the enemy of France.'[11] More constructive perhaps were the professional relationships forged between the National Maritime Museum and French institutions who lent their objects to the exhibition. But Napoleon remains a much more controversial and divisive figure in France than Nelson is in Britain.[12] The conflict between royalist and republican interpretations of French history remained crucial, in the selection of the canon of literature and of historical heroes and villains. In Britain, our sense of history has been more inclusive and pluralist, with erstwhile opponents celebrated for their different and valuable contributions to a shared past. Had the Museum not been bound to an exhibition of six months' duration because of the length of time for which objects are generally lent, more might have been done in partnership to maximize the value of the exhibition from a European perspective. Certainly such arguments add weight to the case for greater collections mobility in Europe.

Audience Reactions

What about the audiences themselves? How did the tens of thousands who visited react to the exhibition? Unfortunately, as with all such events, much of the detailed audience reaction remains unknown except anecdotally. Clearly the poor quality of many of the press reviews did little to keep visitors away, and the fact that so many people came to see it during a very difficult summer for Britain is something to celebrate. However, in addition to undertaking exit polls, the Museum maintains a customer response database compiled from the feedback forms available for completion in its galleries. Nearly 3,000 of the 91,000 visitors completed a form. A mere 9 per cent of the feedback was critical, 63 per cent was complimentary, and the remainder of the responses consisted of questions or comments about the Museum in general. A recurrent theme was the sheer comprehensiveness of the exhibition, and people certainly appreciated seeing loans from France alongside objects from our national collection. Numbers of respondents

---

[11] *France Magazine*, 1 September 2005, 8.
[12] See also Peter Hicks, Chapter 7 below.

noted how much they had learned and how instructive the exhibition was. One person commented, 'I particularly appreciated the development of the context of the French Revolution, which I had never understood before.' Another wrote, 'For the first time I really understood why Trafalgar was such an important battle, even though it didn't topple Napoleon.' Several commented that the presentation of the two men made it easier to understand the rivalry between France and England. One such comment reads, 'I realize how deep and far reaching the differences and antipathy are between the French and English.' Many recorded that they had spent several hours looking at the exhibits; others returned more than once. The exhibition also seems to have been successful in stimulating curiosity, and several noted that it had made them wish to find out more—how exactly did Napoleon die? Did anyone find out who shot Nelson? Did the French later regard him as a hero? This kind of comment prompts museums to find mechanisms that will allow the curious to drill down into collections and archives, and ways of better integrating web resources with exhibitions so that visitors can continue their enquiries at home. Of course, some locals simply viewed the exhibition as an opportunity for veneration: an exhibition that makes one 'proud to be British', or even 'proud to be English', found its way onto several comment cards. But many respondents noted that the exhibition was balanced and without bias, although French visitors were more likely to find that references to Nelson's battles were nationalistic and to claim that the Museum had applied a British 'gloss' to matters Napoleonic. At least the title and bilingual captions did attract more French visitors to the Museum than would otherwise have been the case. Many found the experience poignant, and several admitted to having been moved to tears. It is impossible to generalize from feedback offered by such a self-selected group, yet the value of the exhibition in stimulating curiosity and even a desire for further debate is undeniable. 'Makes me want to learn more about this period of history' was a typical comment.

Since thousands of visitors viewed the exhibition in spite of the bombings, the importance of exhibitions in the construction of the past is significant, especially taking into account the related publicity, which would have been at least registered by a still wider audience. The exhibition also attracted an audience from a wider socio-economic base than is currently usual for museums, proving that if the subject has mass appeal, a museum venue is not necessarily a barrier to engagement.

The exhibition's intellectual legacy is nevertheless difficult to gauge so soon after the event. Exhibition catalogues have some permanence but exhibitions themselves provide a brief snapshot of historical opinion at a certain point in time. Nevertheless, they are surely proper objects of historiographical enquiry. The objects on display did give French and British viewers an opportunity to gain a better historic understanding of why relations between the two countries continue to be so ambivalent. One noted that it offered 'an experience enabling me to appreciate history and its effect on our present world'. Another commented that it 'made me understand the importance Nelson and Napoleon had in shaping the modern face of Europe'. Exhibitions can also bring history to life. One person wrote, 'This is great! Before visiting I had no idea of how interesting and exciting naval history can be. Thank you.'

Conclusion

Public response to the 2005 anniversary suggests that Britain is at last beginning to take its maritime heritage more seriously. The process will continue, with the vexed question of how to interpret the abolition of the slave trade in 1807 (with its obvious maritime dimension) and the 150th anniversary of the Indian Mutiny (where troop ships were so important in carrying men to the subcontinent). Public history has never been more important. What should be commemorated, and in what manner, raises highly contentious and significant questions not only about definitions of leadership, but also of national identity and citizenship. Politicians of all parties have been debating the question, and for many school students history is a means of informing them about the nature of their multicultural society, and its complex relations with other parts of the world.

7.
The Battle of Austerlitz, Collective Amnesia, and the Non-Commemoration of Napoleon in France

PETER HICKS

This essay is a meditation upon the absence of official commemoration in France of the Napoleonic bicentenaries—an absence set in high relief by the relatively high-profile official ceremonies organized in Britain for the year 2005 and the commemoration (and celebration) of Trafalgar. While French official reticence had already been noticeable in 1996, the anniversary of Napoleon's First Italian Campaign, it was most apparent in 2005. The French press deplored official reluctance to commemorate France's (and Napoleon's) greatest military victory at Austerlitz on 2 December 1805, which was made particularly striking by the presence in June that year of the French president, Jacques Chirac, in his official capacity, at a re-enactment of Trafalgar in the Solent aboard France's largest aircraft carrier, *Charles de Gaulle*. Britain was not alone in its fairly comfortable attitude to bicentenaries of the Napoleonic period. In the Czech Republic, on 2 December 2005, thousands of history enthusiasts converged on the small village of Slavkov to re-enact and remember the epoch-making Battle of Austerlitz. It is true that the French defence minister put in an appearance on the day. Madame Michèle Alliot-Marie, accompanied both by a Czech delegation and by the band of the École d'application de l'artillerie de Draguignan, spent the day on the battlefield and made two official appearances. The first was on the site of Napoleon's headquarters on the Žuran hillock, where she made a speech and performed an act of remembrance; at the second, in the company of Russian and Austrian delegations, she laid a wreath on the Peace Monument, which had been placed there in 1905:

> We are here today to commemorate this both tragic and fascinating event in the history of Europe. . . . And this is not out of a need to glorify war, but rather from a desire to give just homage, from across the centuries, to all those who shed their blood for their homelands. . . . As a result of this event of world renown, Europeans have had a chance to remember together the

price of peace and to feel the real value of a democratic, free, and secure Europe.[1]

But this was not enough to satisfy either contributors to French newspapers such as *Le Monde*, *Le Figaro*, and *Libération* in December 2005, or the Napoleonistic public. Even the parallel event that took place in the Place Vendôme, Paris, was seen as 'too little, too late'. Here Monsieur Pascal Clément, Justice minister, presided over a commemoration of the bicentenary of the victory at Austerlitz, in the presence of General Henri Bentegeat, chef d'état-major des armées, and General Bernard Thorette, chef d'état-major de l'armée de terre. This involved a historical 'évocation' performed by a battalion from the École spéciale militaire de Saint-Cyr, and included the use of standards and flags of the regiments of the French army which had fought in the Battle of Austerlitz. Also present were representatives of all the countries of the EU, Russia, and the USA.[2] The biggest bugbear for critics was that the French head of state was absent. President Jacques Chirac's official agenda obliged him to be in Bamako, Mali, at the Africa–France summit. And Prime Minister Dominique de Villepin—despite his professed interest in things Napoleonic[3]—was away in Amiens. To the media, it looked as if the high officers of state were boycotting the event. Seeking possible reasons for official embarrassment con-

---

[1] The full speech cited on the French defence ministry website: www.defense.gouv.fr/sites/defense/decouverte/le_ministere/ministre_de_la_defense/declarations/2005/decembre/commemoration_du_bicentenaire_dausterlitz_le_021205 (accessed 21 July 2006) reads as follows: 'Nous sommes réunis aujourd'hui pour commémorer cet événement à la fois tragique et fascinant de l'histoire de l'Europe. Depuis plusieurs décennies, la reconstitution de la bataille d'Austerlitz rassemble en Moravie du Sud plusieurs dizaines de milliers d'hommes et de femmes, venus d'Europe et du monde entier. Férus d'histoire, de stratégie militaire, ils se réunissent en ces lieux, sur le Plateau de Pratzen et aux alentours. Ils sont animés, non du besoin de glorifier la guerre, mais de la volonté de rendre un juste hommage, à travers les siècles, à tous ceux qui ont versé ici leur sang, pour leur patrie. Deux cents ans plus tard, les adversaires d'hier sont les amis d'aujourd'hui. Les combats et les rivalités ont laissé la place à la réconciliation et à une paix durable entre les peuples européens. L'Europe, aujourd'hui une puissance économique, de plus en plus une puissance politique, offre au monde l'image exemplaire d'une union des peuples œuvrant ensemble à la liberté et la paix. Cette manifestation est une occasion de célébrer les valeurs communes qui animent désormais nos démocraties. C'est un signe d'espoir fort pour tous les pays qui aujourd'hui encore s'affrontent par les armes. Je tiens à saluer l'action de celles et ceux qui chaque année permettent à des dizaines de milliers d'Européens de commémorer ensemble cette page de leur Histoire, notamment les autorités de la région de Moravie du sud, la Central European Napoleonic Society ou l'association des vingt communes du champ de bataille. Grâce à cette manifestation de renommée mondiale, les Européens ont une occasion de se souvenir ensemble du prix de la paix, de la valeur d'une Europe démocratique, libre et sûre.'

[2] Communiqué from the French Ministry of Defence at: www.defense.gouv.fr/sites/defense/base/breves/bicentenaire_de_la_victoire_dausterlitz.

[3] Dominique de Villepin, *Les Cent-Jours ou l'esprit de sacrifice* (Paris, 2001).

cerning Napoleon (and nationalist sentiment), some journalists cited the fortnight-long rioting among France's ethnic minorities in the summer of 2005. Others noted the provocative publication on 1 December 2005 of the vitriolic (and historically flawed) pamphlet comparing the treatment of slaves in Santo Domingo during the First Empire with genocide, and Napoleon with Hitler.[4] Interior minister Nicolas Sarkozy complained of a certain political correctness, whereby France appeared continually to be apologizing for her history.[5]

However, the causes of official commemorative reticence were much more deep-rooted. Writing in *Le Monde*, philosopher Nicolas Castoldi touched on French ambivalence regarding Napoleon:

> Napoleon embodies the contradictions of his times: the Revolution, her grandeur, but also her failures, and the long and painful problematic concerning her end. Even before Napoleon emerged from behind Bonaparte, the Revolutionary wars were both necessary in defence of the endangered fatherland and an opportunity to export the new democracy to Europe. Napoleon is the expression of his period, just as de Gaulle was one century later. None of this is especially contentious, but you cannot have one side of the history without the other. As Clemenceau used to say: 'The Revolution is a single block.'[6]

Note the principal terms of contrast used here: 'contradictions', 'one side [against] the other', 'grandeur' and 'failure', 'Bonaparte' and 'Napoleon'.[7] Napoleon remains a problematic figure in France. And so despite initial plans, there was in the end no major Austerlitz exhibition at the Paris Musée de l'Armée, nor was there a major public debate. Clearly there had been no political will to go any further, nor did there appear to be any political capital to be gained from investing in Napoleonic commemorations. Hence, while France's European partners were able to commemorate

---

[4] Claude Ribbe, *Le Crime de Napoléon* (Paris, 2005).

[5] French television channel, Tf1 (11 December 2005). Remarking upon French 'embarrassment' regarding the commemoration of the victory at Austerlitz, Nicolas Sarkozy stated that 'our society is threatened by an appalling tendency of denial of self'. 'Shall we end up one day apologizing for being French?', he asked, before people finally 'face up to' ('assumer sans complaisance') the history of France, 'but without excessively apologizing' ('excès de repentance'). Quoted at: http://ameliefr.club.fr.

[6] *Le Monde*, 20 December 2005.

[7] In his *Grand Dictionnaire Universel du XIXe siècle* (Paris, 1866–79), Pierre Larousse enshrined this Bonaparte–Napoleon dichotomy by giving two entries for the Consul and Emperor. The former begins: 'Bonaparte — the greatest, most glorious, most brilliant name in history, even including Napoleon, general of the French Republic, born in Ajaccio (Island of Corsica) on 15 August 1769, who died in the Château de Saint-Cloud, near Paris, on 18 Brumaire an VIII.' The latter reads: 'Napoleon I, Emperor of the French . . . political and military dictator and imitator of the Caesars.'

Napoleon—of course without forgetting certain national sensitivities—as an integral part of common modern European roots, France herself was unable to grasp the nettle. The reaction in hard-core Napoleonic circles was predictably scathing:

> Our Republic has just given the most 'disparaging' (*dévalorisante*) image possible of its history. By not appearing at the different commemorations marking the bicentenary of the victory at Austerlitz, the President of the Republic and his Prime Minister have failed in their duty. And this is even less excusable given that several weeks earlier, France had joined in the grandiose English celebrations related to the bicentenary of the defeat of the French navy at Trafalgar! And just to give the right tone, President Chirac sent our aircraft carrier, *Charles de Gaulle*, the jewel of our national navy. So now, nothing is too grand when it is a question of commemorating our defeats! This is the appalling impression left by this refusal to participate in the homage to all the soldiers, of all nations, who died on the field of honour at Austerlitz on 2 December 1805. Neither the French nation nor the French army deserved such an affront.[8]

This tirade however is not just a *cri de coeur* regarding the non-celebration of Austerlitz. For French Napoleonists this forgetfulness goes against one of their fundamental tenets of belief, namely, that of remembering. And this 'memorial' tradition was begun by Napoleon himself. He built his very existence upon it, and this was picked up and developed by his supporters and enthusiasts through subsequently created Napoleonic 'realms of memory' ('lieux de mémoire'). Pierre Nora defines 'les lieux de mémoire' as 'not what we remember but the place where memory works, not the tradition itself but its laboratory'.[9] Throughout his life the emperor himself was interested in history and the writing of history. When Napoleon came to power he was conscious of his position within history as a whole, hence his obsession with writing accounts of his deeds

---

[8] 'Notre république vient de donner au monde l'image la plus dévalorisante qui soit sur son histoire. En s'abstenant de paraître aux différentes commémorations marquant le bicentenaire de la Victoire d'Austerlitz, le président de la république et son Premier ministre ont failli à leur devoir. Cela est d'autant moins excusable que, quelques semaines auparavant, la France s'était associée aux grandioses festivités anglaises se rapportant au bicentenaire de la défaite de la marine française à Trafalgar! Le président Chirac, pour faire bonne figure, y envoya jusqu'à notre porte-avions Charles de Gaulle, joyau de notre marine nationale. Rien n'est désormais trop grand pour commémorer nos défaites! C'est la pénible impression qui se dégage après ce refus de participer à l'hommage de tous les soldats, de toutes les nations, tombés au champ d'Honneur à Austerlitz, le 2 décembre 1805. Pas plus que la nation, l'armée française ne méritait un tel affront.' Published on http://ameliefr.club.fr/index-france.html but later removed.

[9] Pierre Nora (ed.), *Les Lieux de Mémoire*, 3 vols (Paris, 1997), vol. 1, pp. 17–18; see also pp. 15 f.

(he made four attempts, for example, to write the perfect account of the Battle of Marengo), with writing in general, and with remembering. He even organized some of the first modern re-enactments. Two examples, one from the very start of the First Empire and the other from the very end, show just how much importance Napoleon attributed to such matters as a means of establishing the identities of his successive regimes. The first came as Napoleon was laying the foundations of his imperial legitimacy in the early summer of 1805. After his coronation in Milan as 'King of Italy', he passed on to the important garrison town of Alessandria, where five years earlier the proto-First Consul had won his first most important military (and propaganda) victory, Marengo. This time, the recently crowned emperor organized a full-scale re-enactment of that key battle to be performed before him, his consort, Josephine, and impressed locals.[10] The second example is the famous 'Champ de Mai' which, rather like Cambridge May Week, was held, in fact, in June 1815. Here, in an attempt to shore up his wavering 'second coming', Napoleon dug deep into French history to produce a re-enactment of Charlemagne's meeting of 'free men', with its 'military, popular and solemn character'.[11] Thereafter Napoleon conflated re-enactment and remembering in the great texts of Napoleonic orthodoxy, namely, Napoleon's own writings published during his exile on St Helena, and the hagiographies 'written' by Montholon and Las Cases, 'memoirs' and a 'memorial' to the great man.[12] Napoleon had created himself as a French 'realm of memory'.

All this was not lost on the young Louis-Napoléon, the future Napoleon III, as he waited in the wings. Even in its name, his Second Empire was the archetype of backward-looking or historically referential regimes. Founded as it was upon a certain recollection of Napoleon I, the Second Empire was all memory, with its Saint Napoléons, its fifths of May, and seconds of December. The Napoleonic virtues celebrated during the Second Empire became suffused into the Third Republic and later French culture, as Sudhir Hazareesingh has pointed out in *The Legend of Napoleon*.[13]

[10] Jean-Marie René Savary, *Mémoires du duc de Rovigo pour servir à l'histoire de l'empereur Napoléon*, 7 vols, 2nd edn (Paris, 1829), vol. 2, p. 122. See also J. E. Driault, *Napoléon en Italie, 1800–1812* (Paris, 1906), p. 321.

[11] De Villepin, *Cent-Jours*, p. 367, n. 1.

[12] Tristan de Montholon, *Commentaires de Napoléon Ier* (Paris, 1867); id., *Mémoires pour servir à l'histoire de France, sous Napoléon, écrits à Sainte-Hélène par les généraux qui ont partagé sa captivité, et publiés sur les manuscrits entièrement corrigés de la main de Napoléon* (Paris, 1823–25); Emmanuel Las Cases, *Mémorial de Sainte-Hélène ou journal où se trouve consigné, jour par jour, ce qu'a dit et fait Napoléon durant Dix-huit mois* (Paris, 1823). Parts of Montholon's and Las Cases's books were dictated by Napoleon himself.

[13] Sudhir Hazareesingh, *The Legend of Napoleon* (London, 2004), p. 13.

After 1848, millions of voters supported Bonapartism for a range of considerations that included reason and self-interest but also encompassed the memories and mythologies that they had come to associate with Napoleon: the political unity of the nation, the centralization of the state, the modernization of its economy, the promotion of individuals on the basis of merit, and the pursuit of 'grandeur' abroad. Far from abandoning these Napoleonic notions after 1870, France's republican rulers incorporated them into their political discourse and imagery: the imperial legend was thus blended into the French republic's definition of its own ideals. The Napoleonic legend is thus not merely of 'historical' interest; it is a tale about the memory and mythology that continues to underlie modern French identity.

Given this historically deep-rooted and profound memorial context, contemporary French official amnesia is all the more surprising. Perhaps, as indicated before, Napoleonic bicentenaries do not provide enough political capital. Perhaps French politicians are concerned about appearing triumphalist in these days of European partnership. It is possibly felt in French political circles that Napoleon is 'too hot' to handle, someone who could be parodied as 'the dictator's dictator'—a criticism which dates back to Napoleonic times. It is sometimes thought that Napoleon is not viewed as a 'good thing' by the Republican Left but rather a figure more to the taste of the Gaullist Right. And perhaps here is a clue as to the reason for the increasingly peripheral position of Napoleon in the French national psyche. As the twentieth century progressed, with its two catastrophic world wars, French military prowess was continually to the fore, and Napoleon suffered as his fame as man of providence was overtaken by that of Charles de Gaulle: 'De Gaulle now represents a modern version of the "liberal legend" of 1815.'[14] In 1921, in the full flush of victory after the First World War, the centenary of Napoleon's death was commemorated in France with great pomp, and in 1969 the bicentenary of Napoleon's birth was used by President Pompidou as an opportunity to highlight Napoleon's restoration of the dignity of the state and the construction of European unity as a counterpoint to the achievements of Pompidou's Gaullist party.[15] But subsequent historical milestones have been left untouched by the French state: the Brumaire Coup d'état, the Constitution of An VIII, the creation of the Council of State, the founding of the Banque de France, the Germinal Franc, the promulgation of the initially Revolutionary but finally decidedly Napoleonic Code Civil, the creation of the prefectoral corps, the founda-

[14] Hazareesingh, *The Legend of Napoleon*, p. 266.
[15] Ibid., p. 263.

tion of the Empire: all these formative moments in French history have been officially overlooked and left unmarked.

While it is true that there are problems inherent in the practice of state-written and state-celebrated history, and although careful attention must be paid to avoid the pitfalls of collective memory so graphically described by Peter Novick,[16] intelligent commemoration and re-enactment can yield historical insight. To take a Napoleonic example, empathy and real comprehension can come from retracing the heroic forty-eight-hour march of Friand's corps from Vienna to the battlefield of Austerlitz and their participation in some of the day's fiercest fighting, in sleet and sub-zero temperatures. Remembering need not be jingoistic tub-thumping. It *is* possible to 'remember' without 'enthusiasm'. Napoleon should be considered—of course without forgetting certain national sensitivities—as an integral part of our shared European roots. He is not only an object of polemic but an object of history, one to be studied with rigour and openness of spirit. The most important point here (and this is one which is not understood in official Paris) is that such commemorations—which are not, or need not be, celebrations—can only be undertaken in a European context. If war is the continuation of politics by other means, then commemoration is the continuation of history by other means. And as such it is one of the best ways of bringing together and trying to understand the different political conceptions of Europe and European society both two centuries ago and today.

---

[16] 'Collective memory . . . is not just historical knowledge shared by a group. Indeed collective memory is in crucial senses a-historical, even anti-historical. . . . Collective memory simplifies; sees events from a single committed perspective; is impatient with ambiguities of any kind; reduces events to mythic archetypes': P. Novick, *The Holocaust and Collective Memory: The American Experience* (London, 2000), p. 3. Cf. M. Halbwachs, *La Mémoire collective*; work published posthumously by Mme Jeanne Halbwachs Alexandre (Paris, 1950).

Index